Thanksgiving Coloring Book

CELEBRATE TRADITIONAL AMERICAN
VALUES WITH THESE 30 DETAILED,
HAND-DRAWN COLORING PAGES
(FOR KIDS & ADULTS)

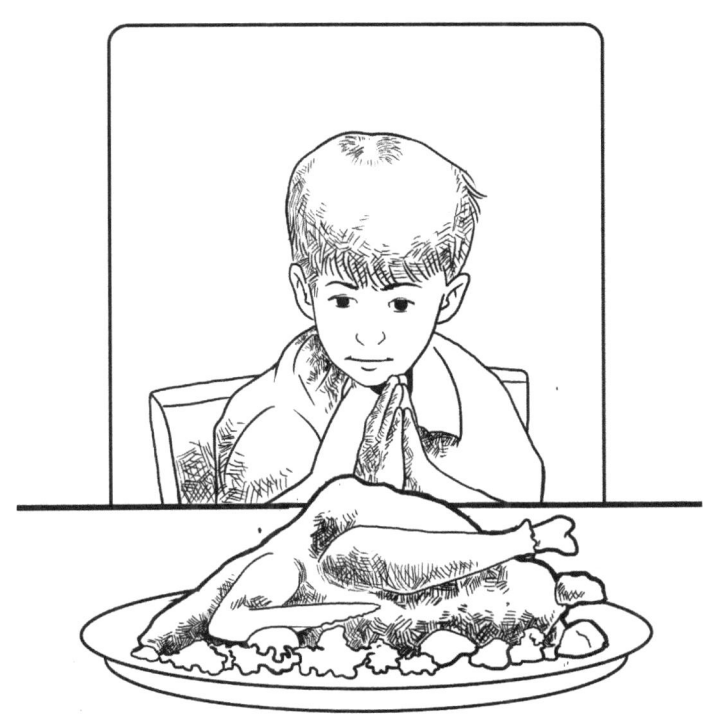

© BONDOLFI BOOKS

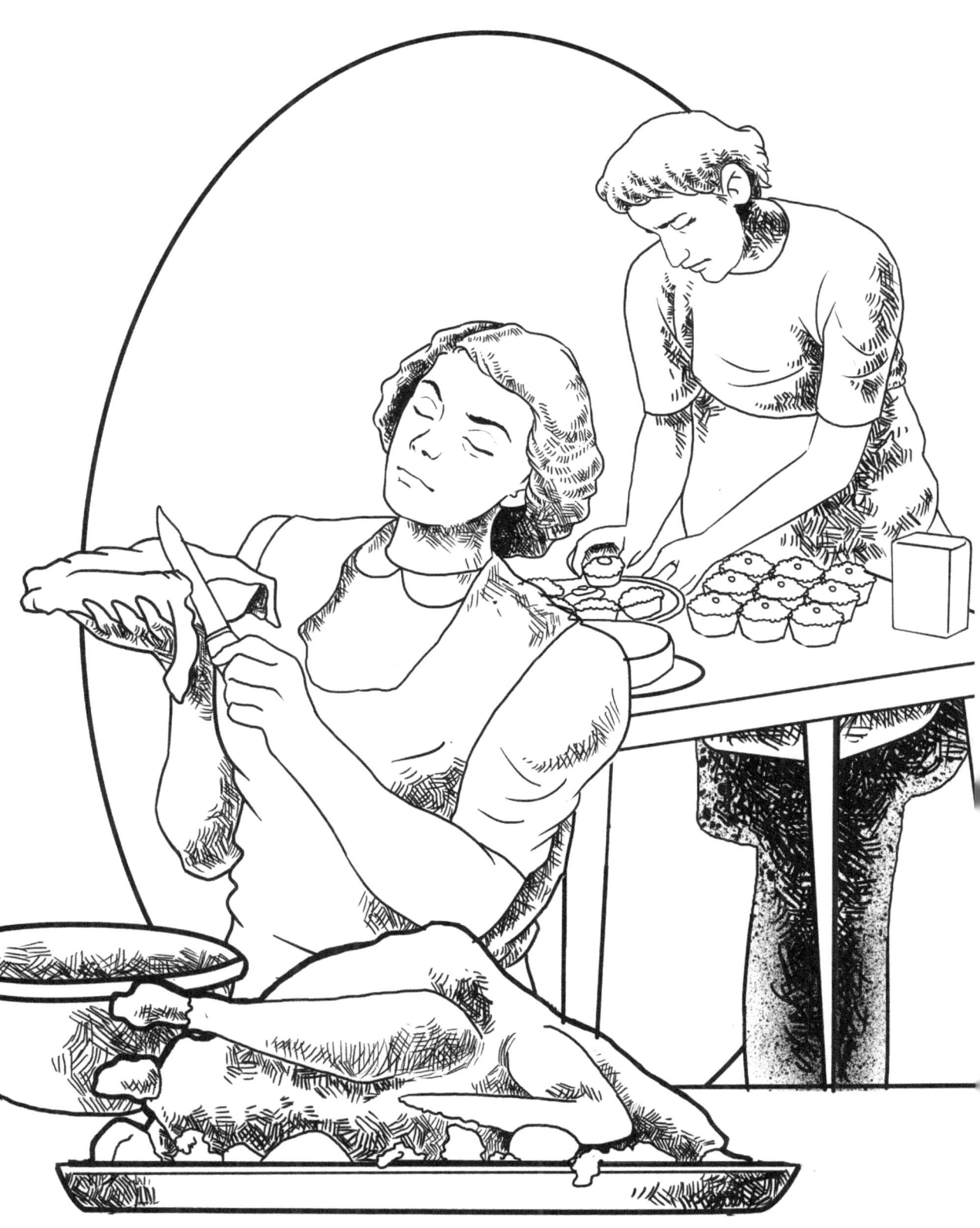

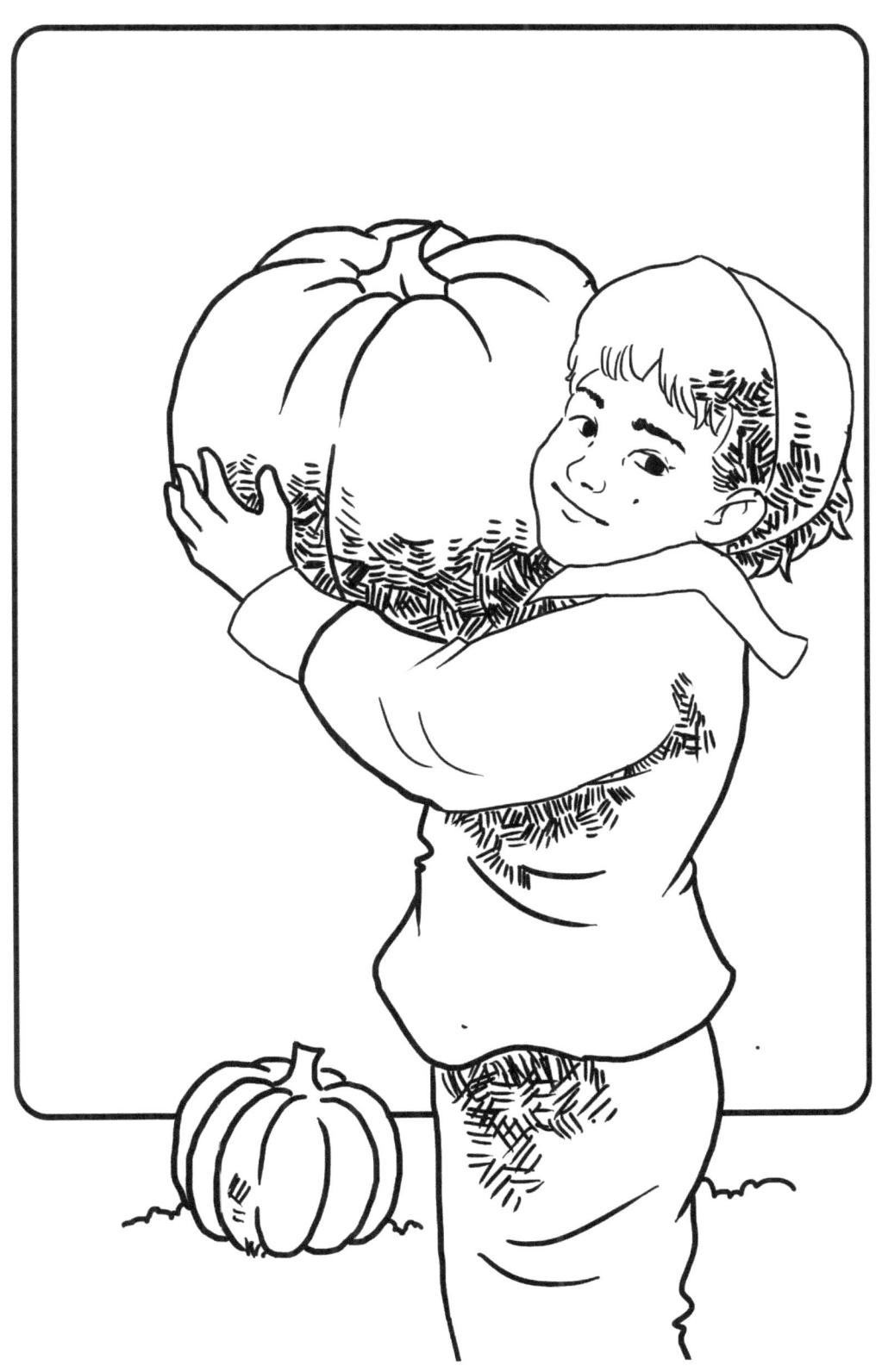

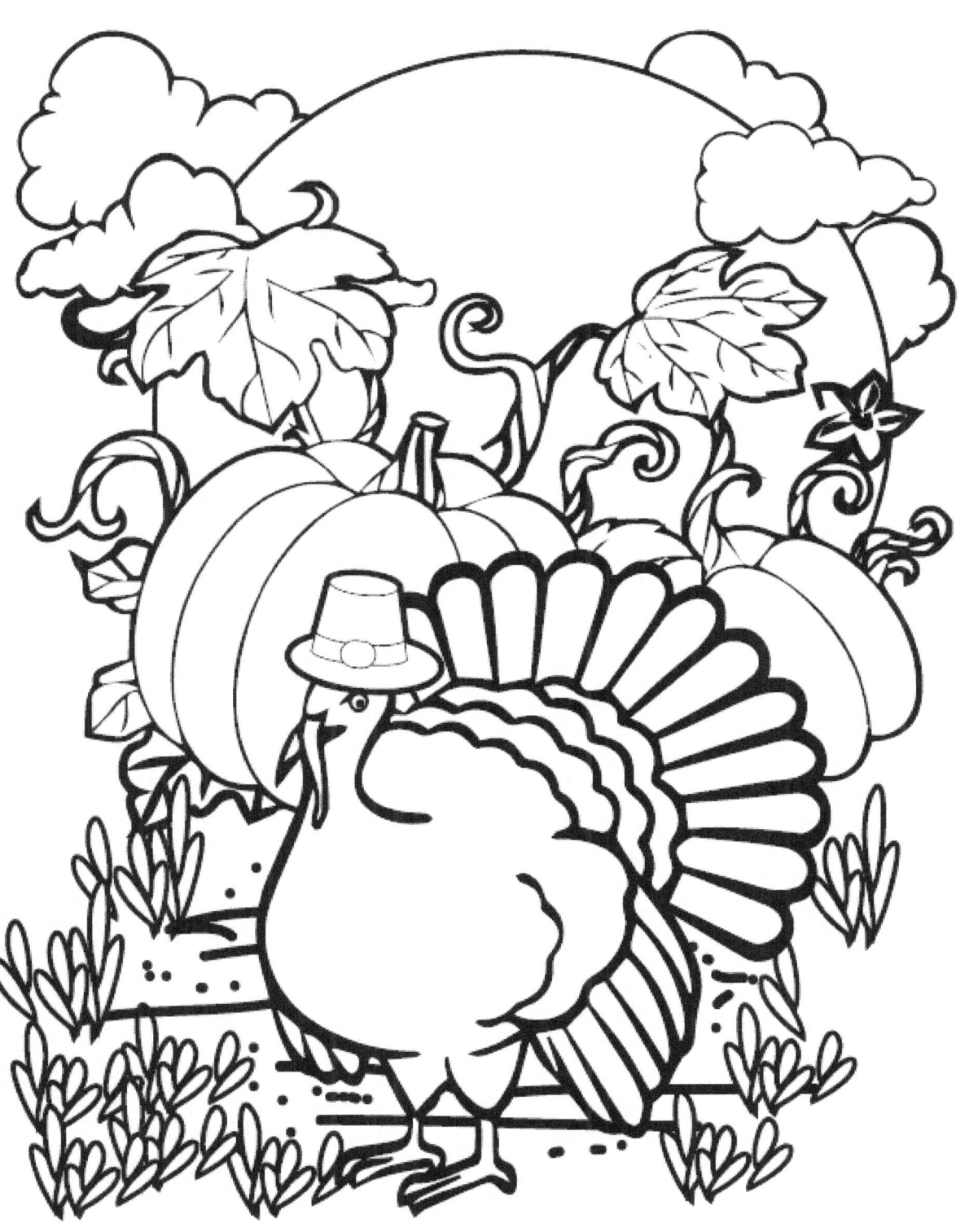

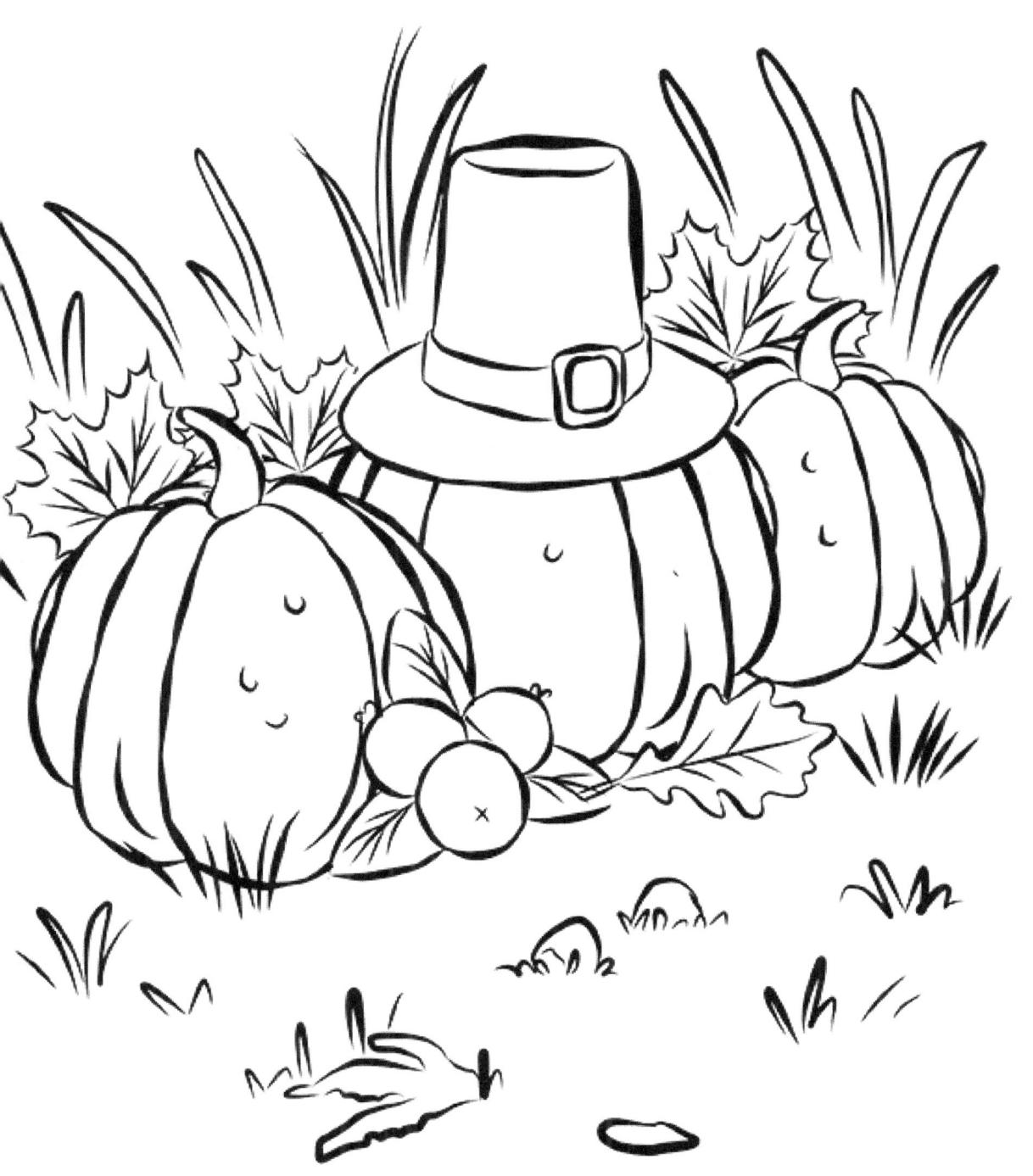

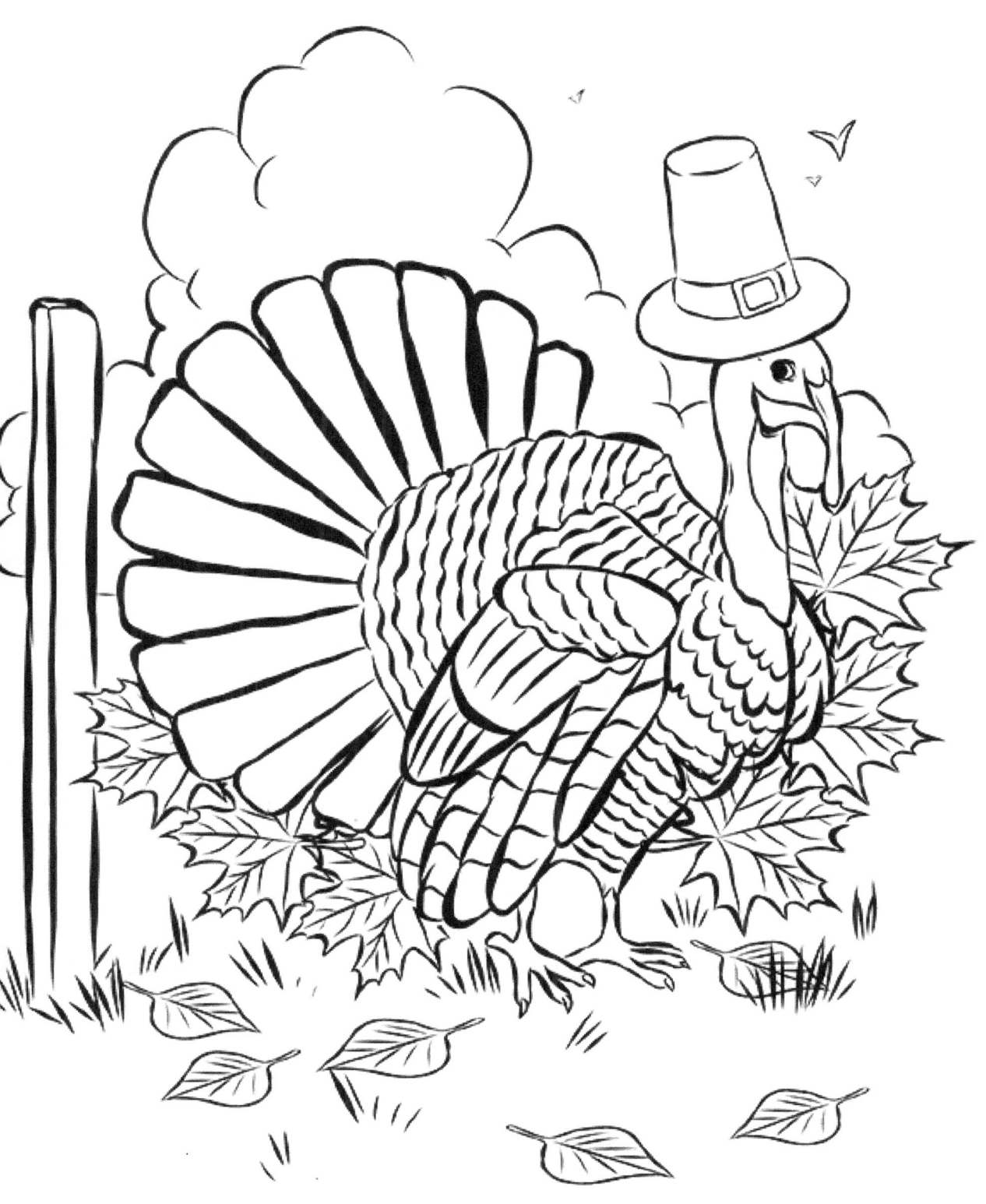

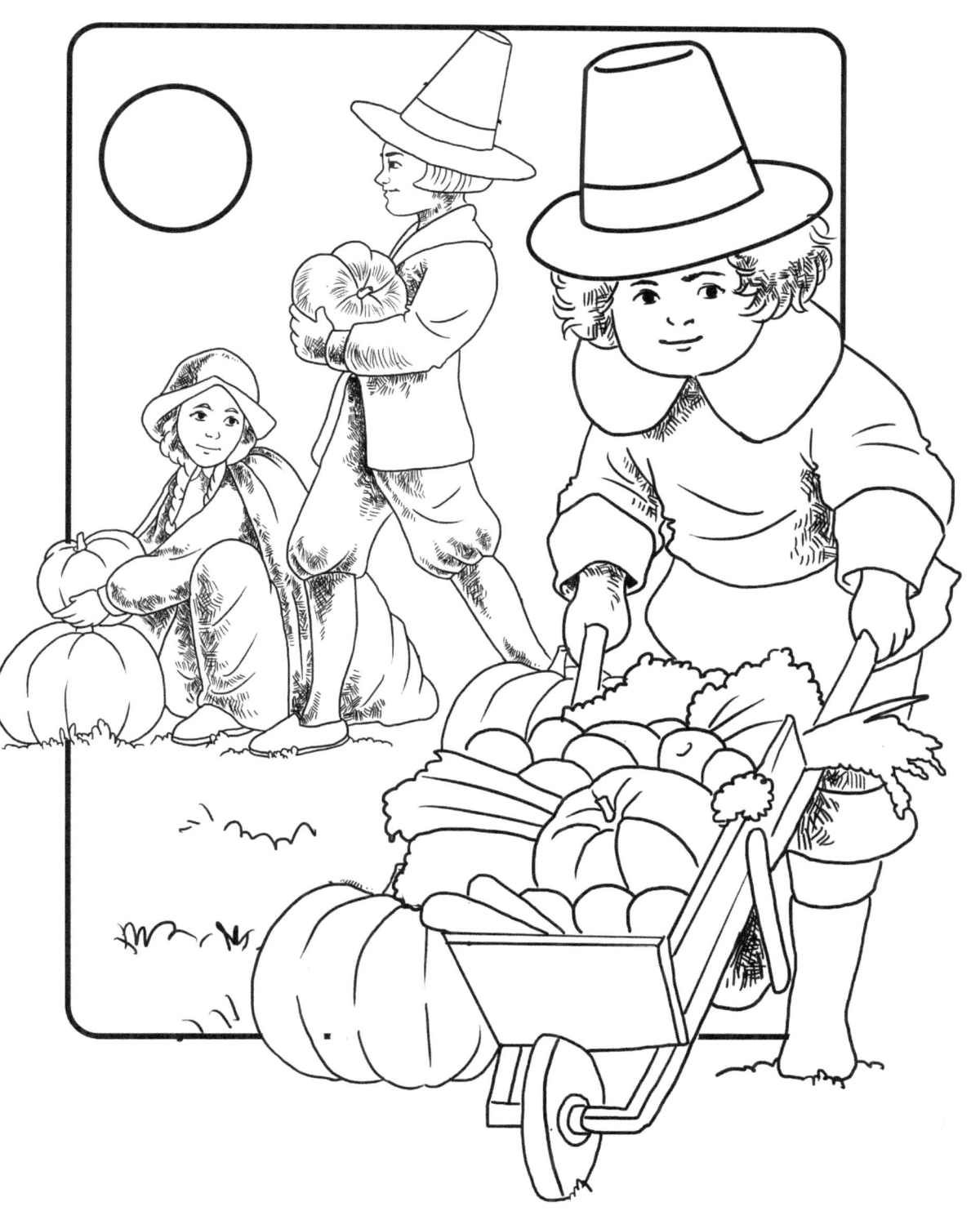

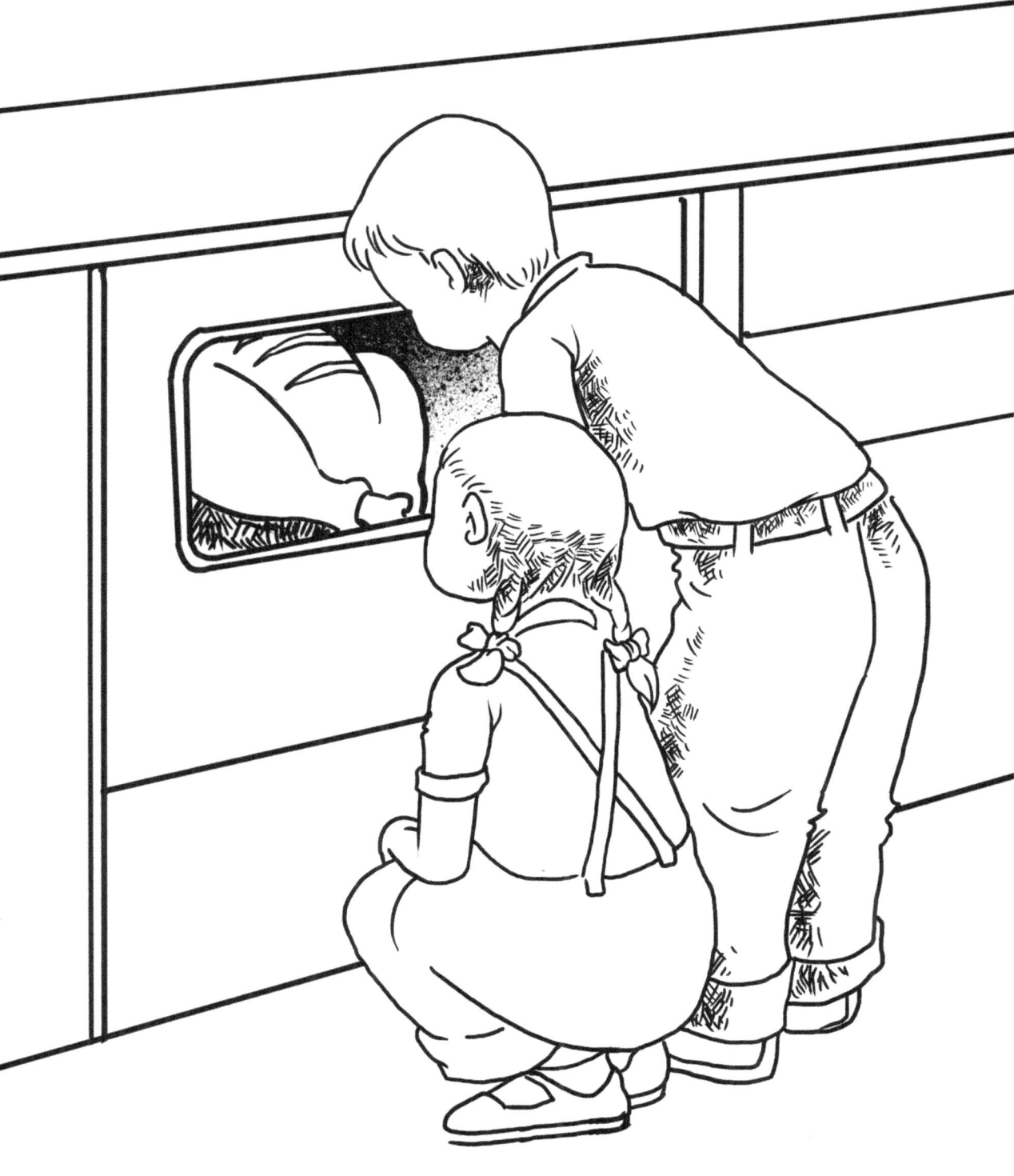

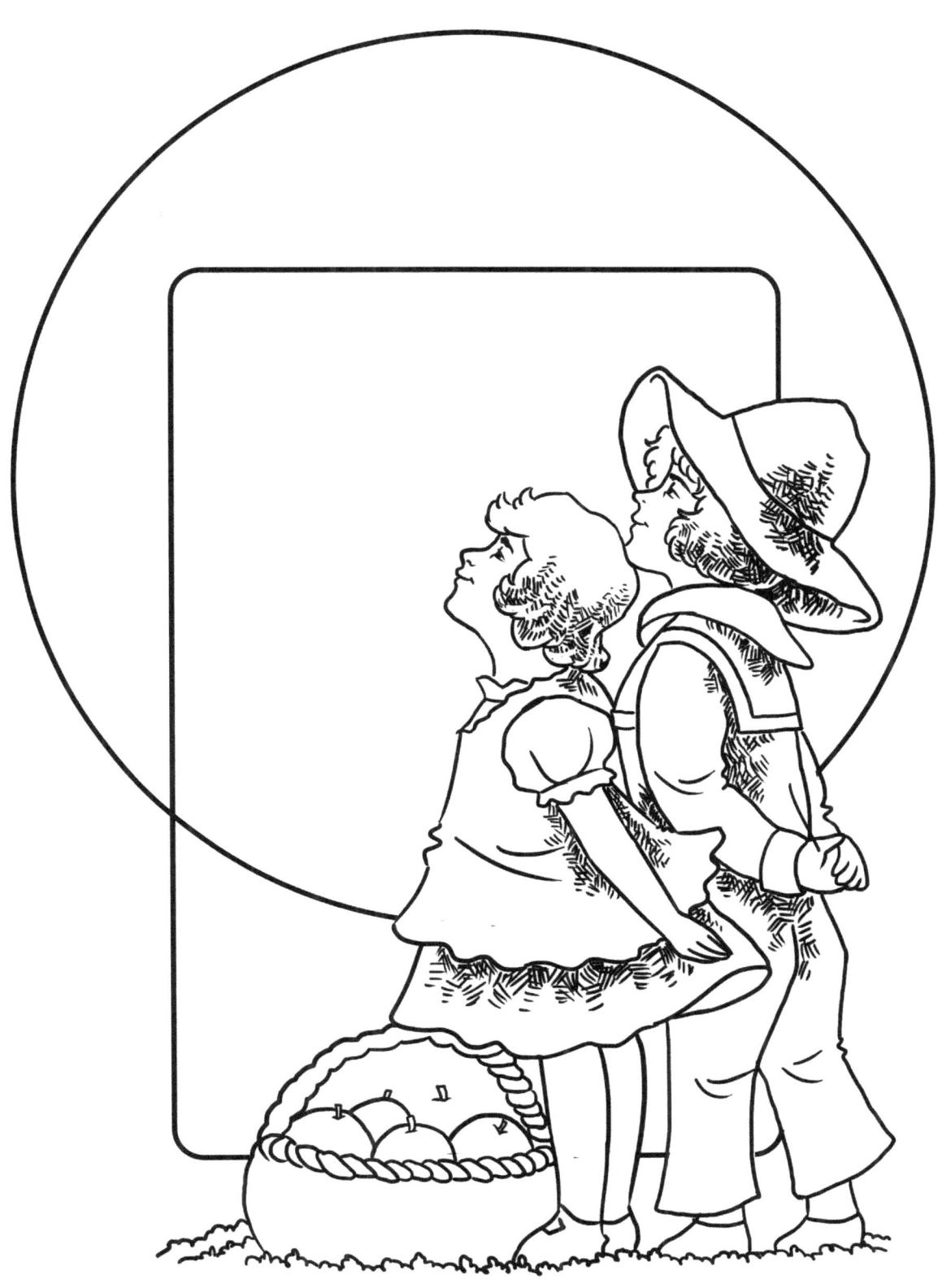

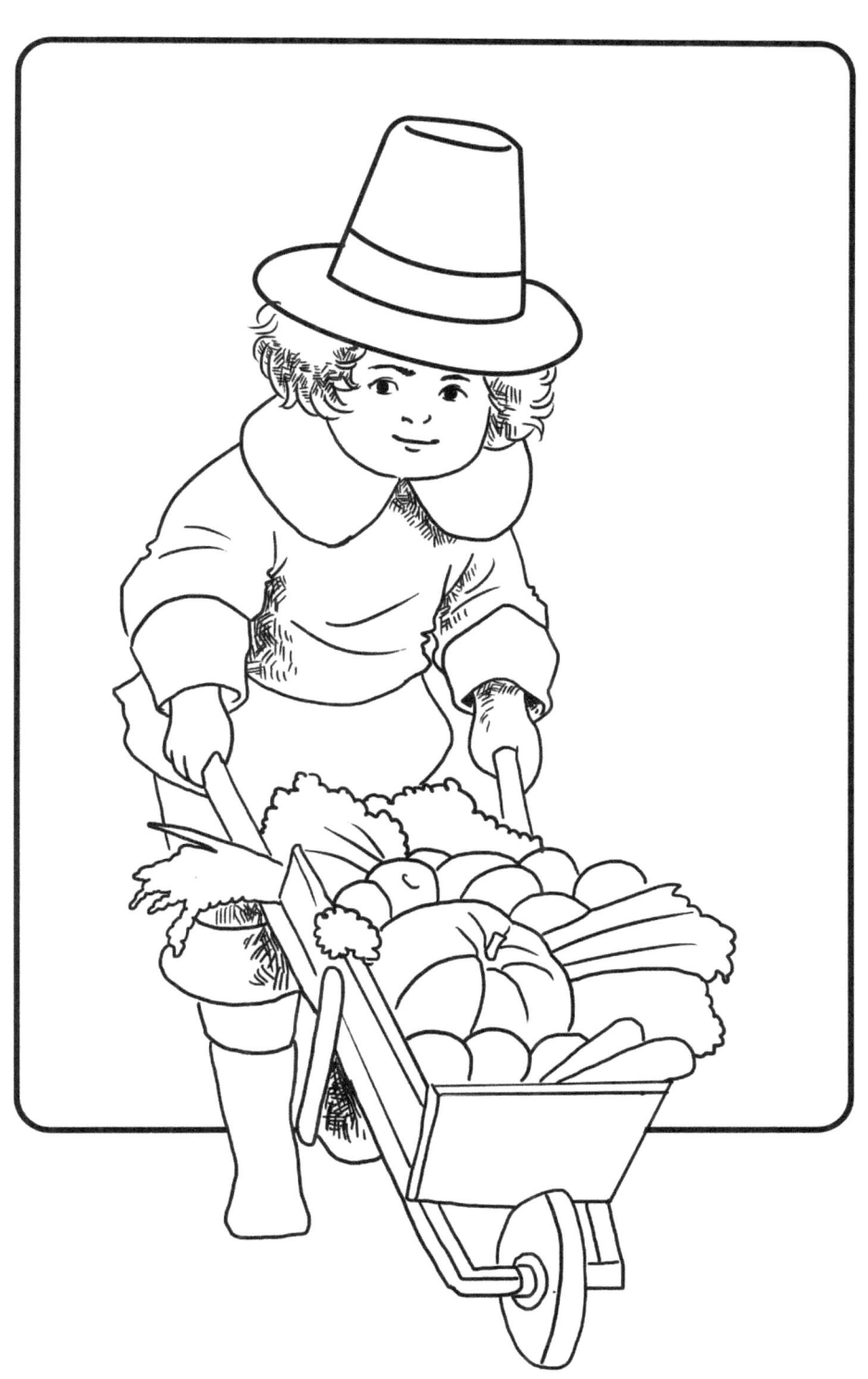

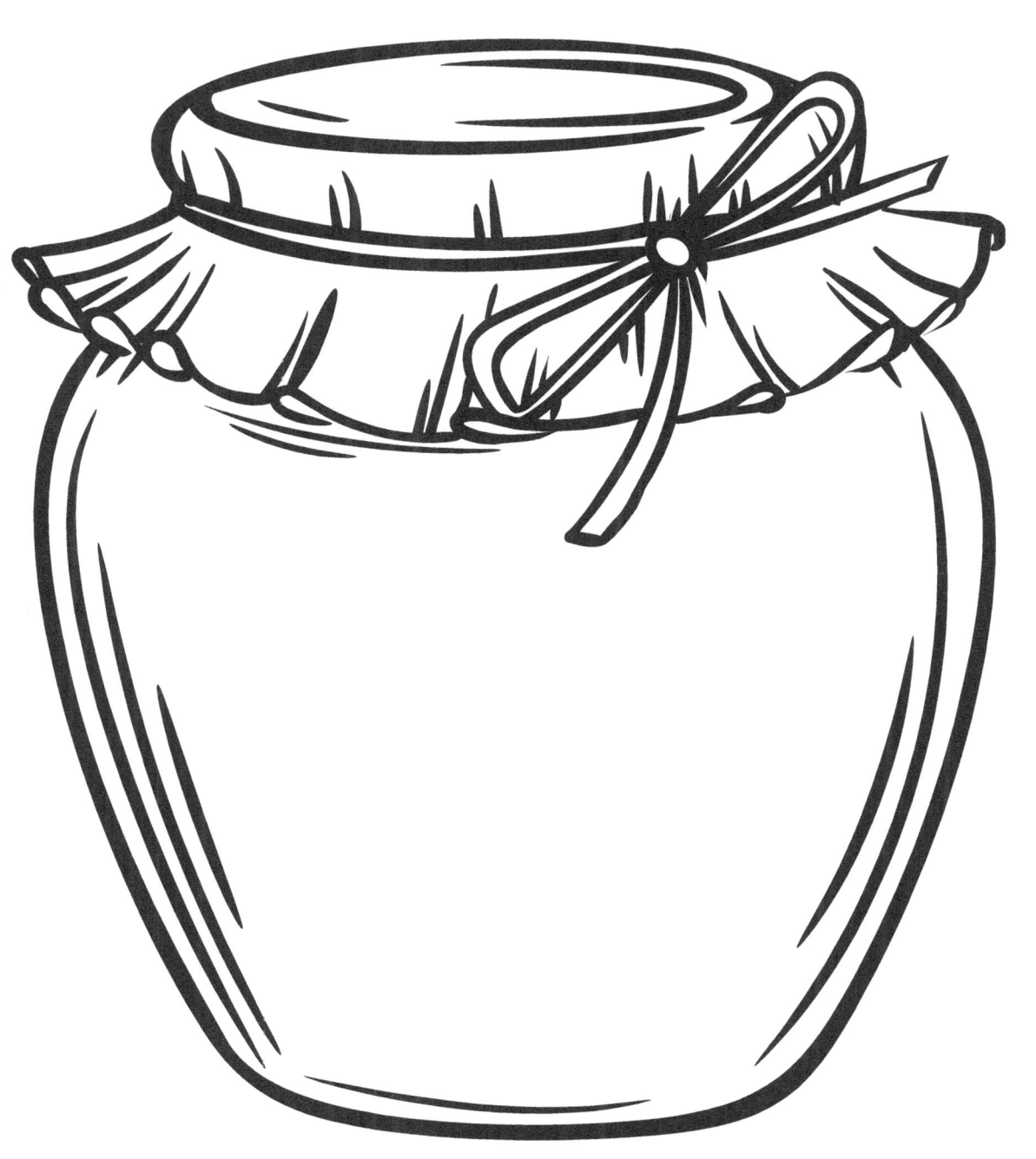

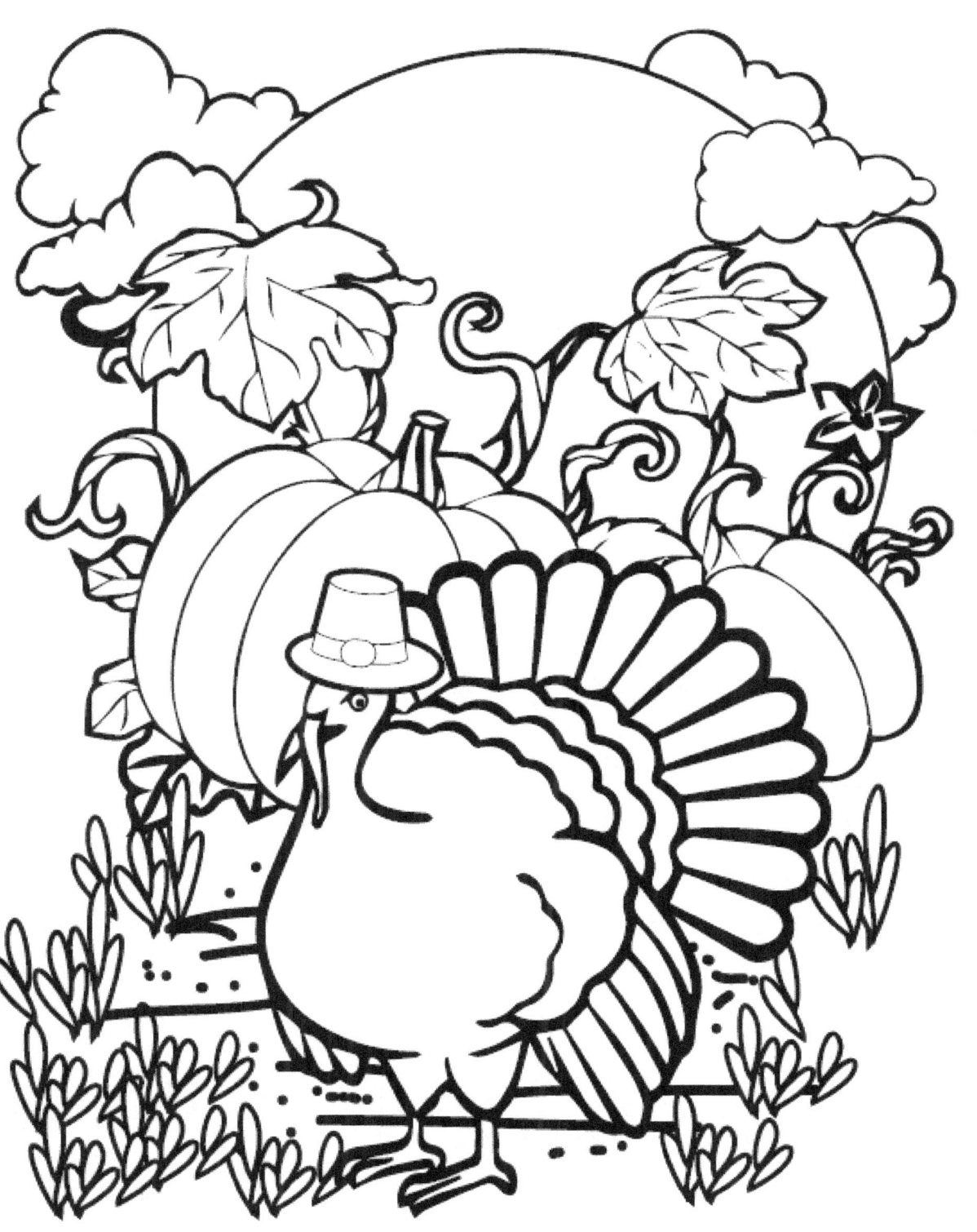

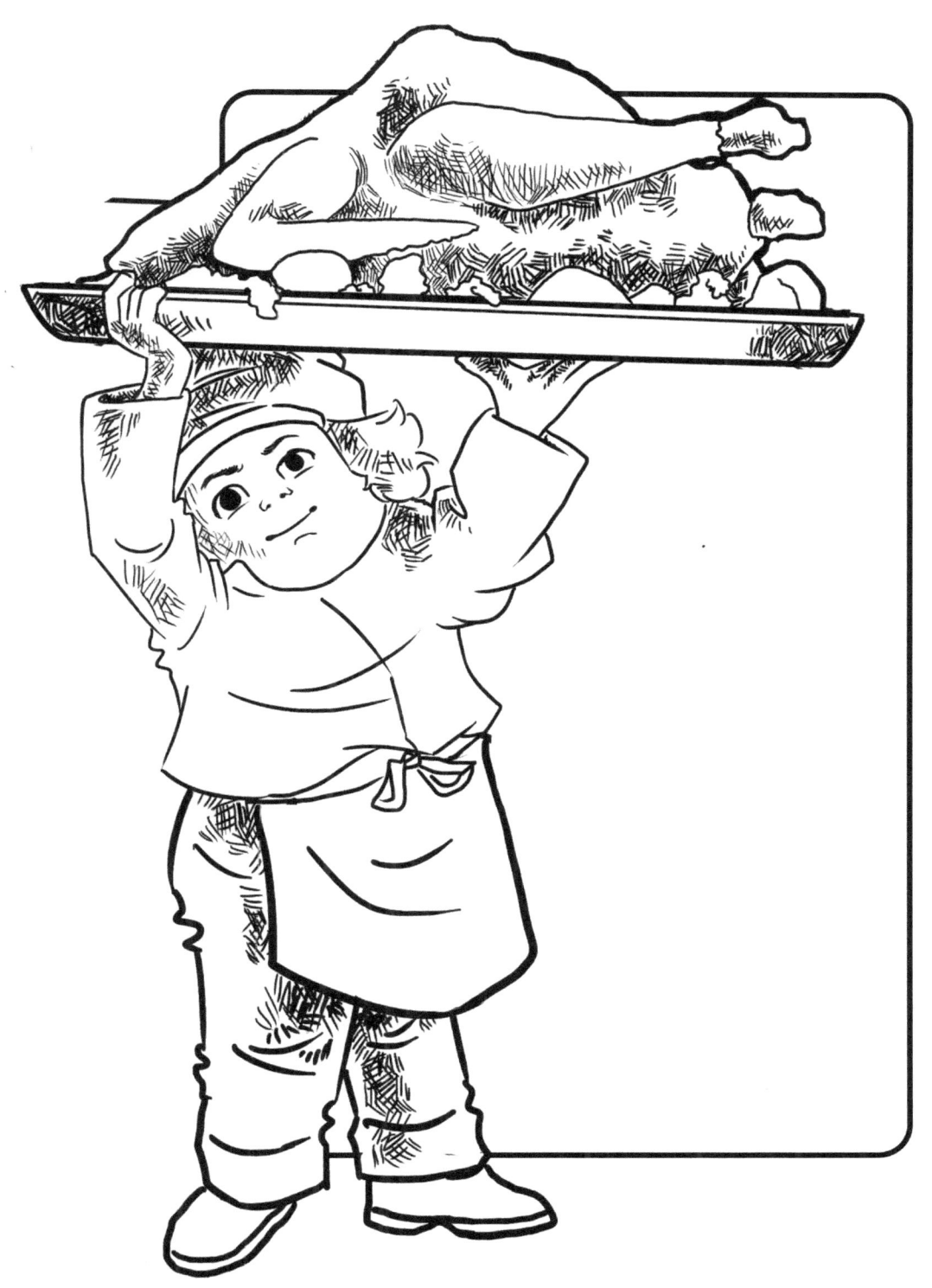

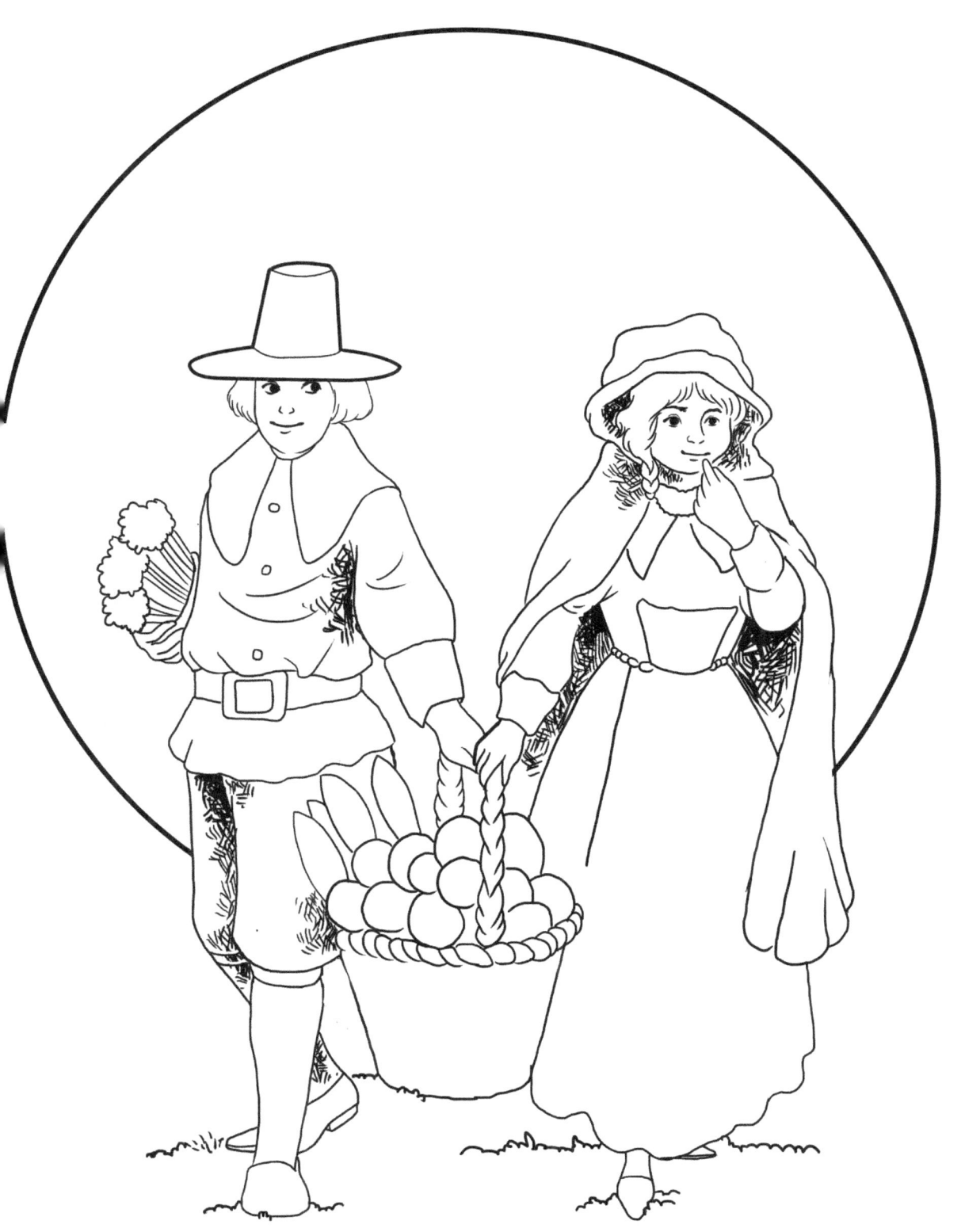

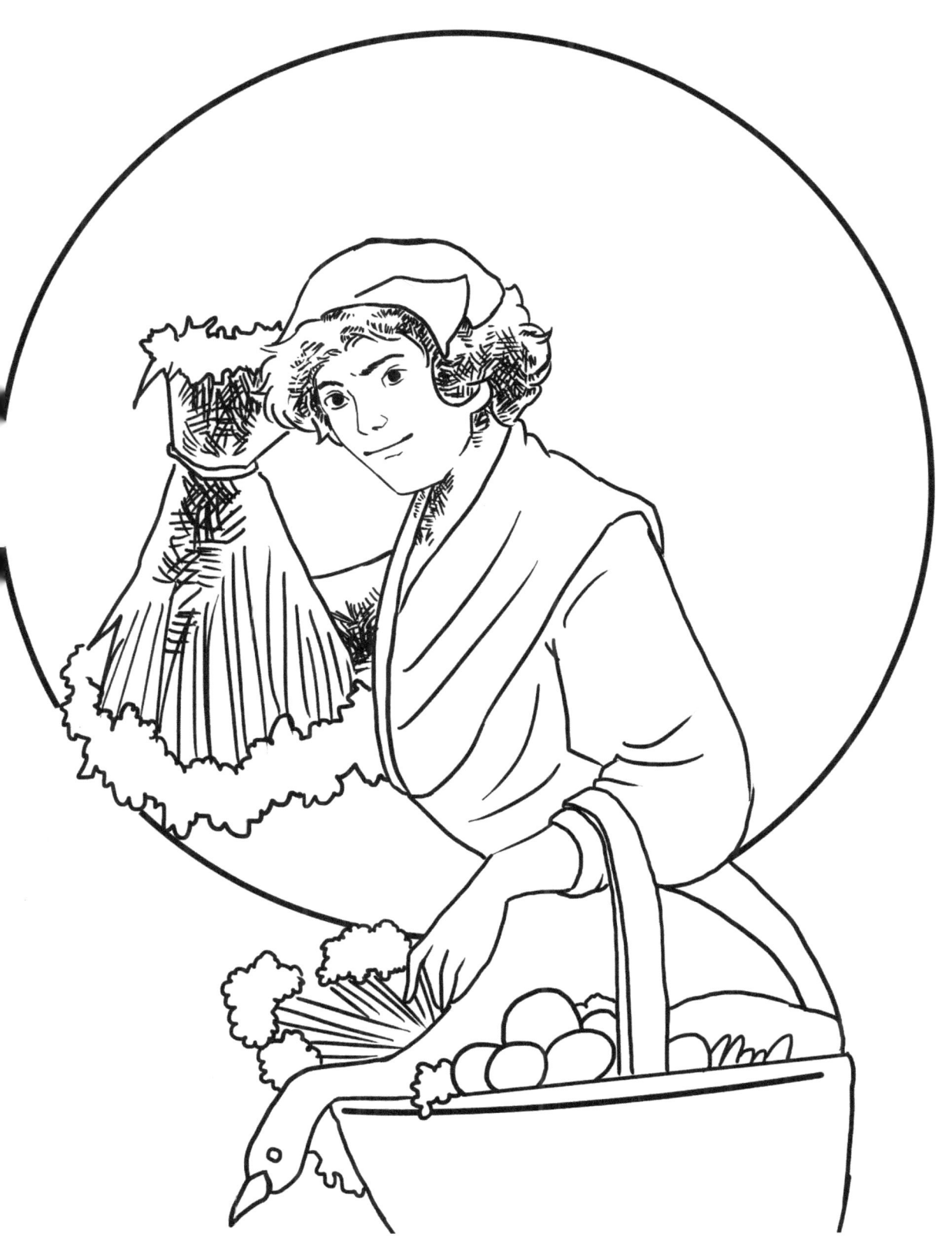

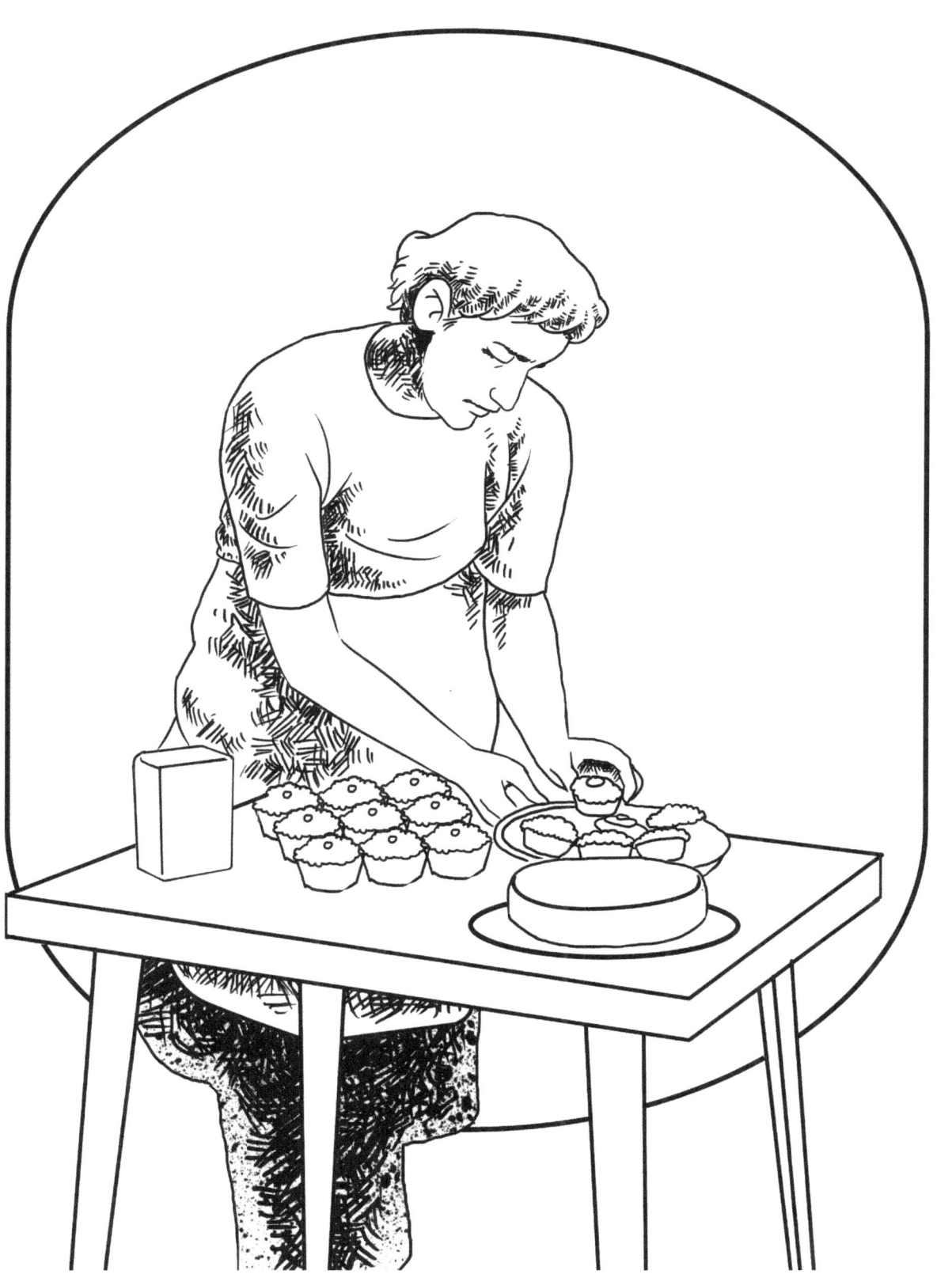

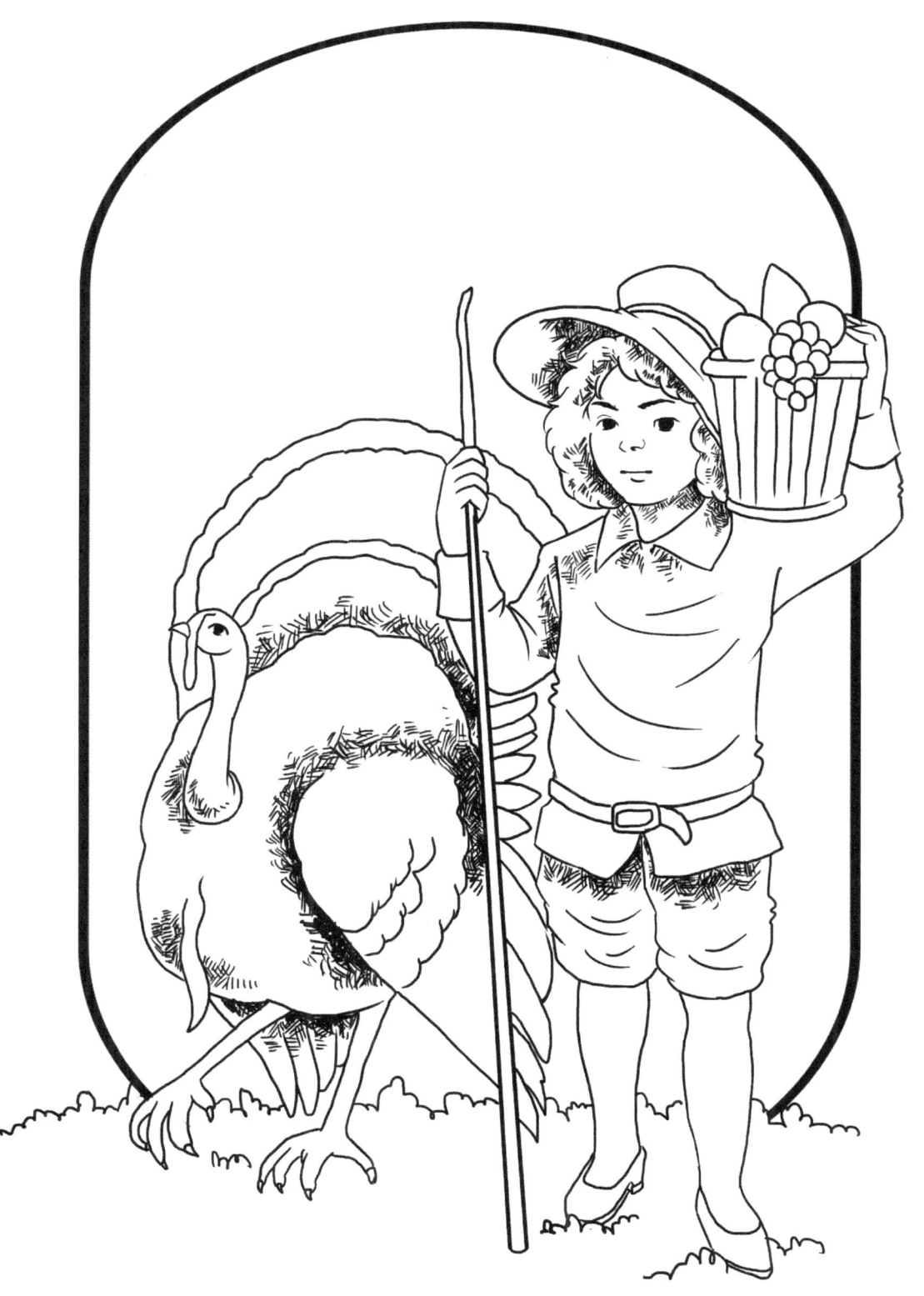

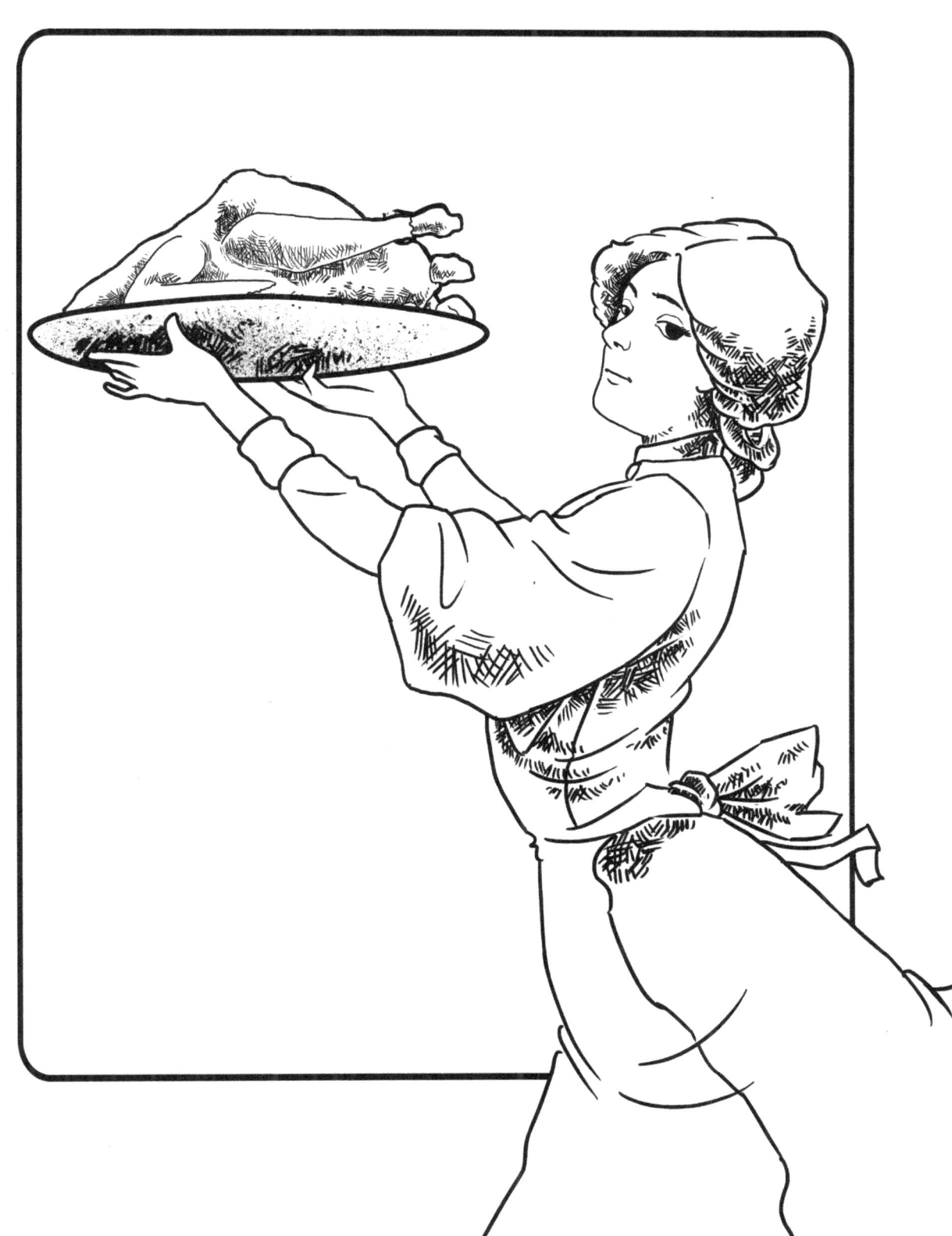

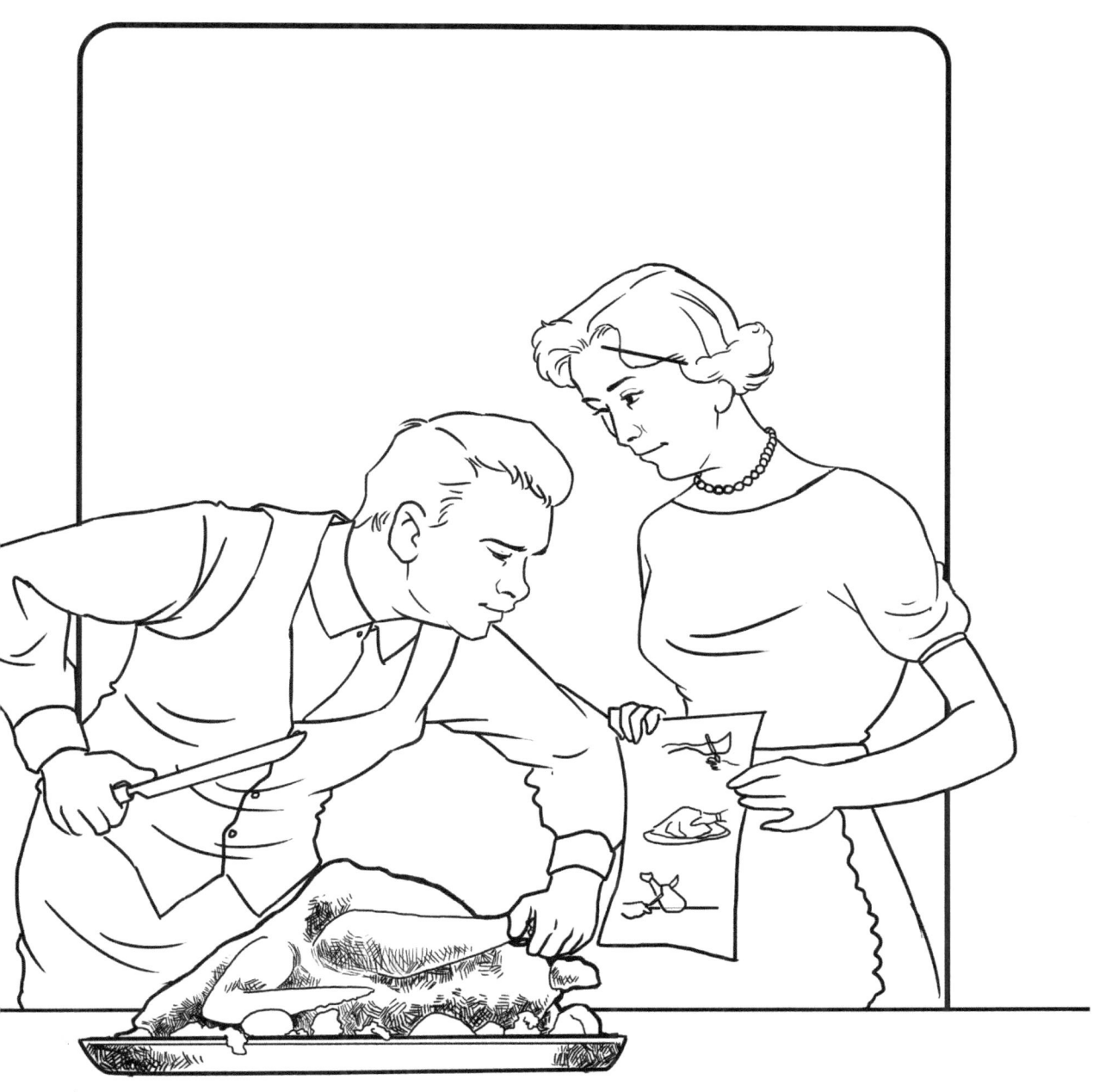

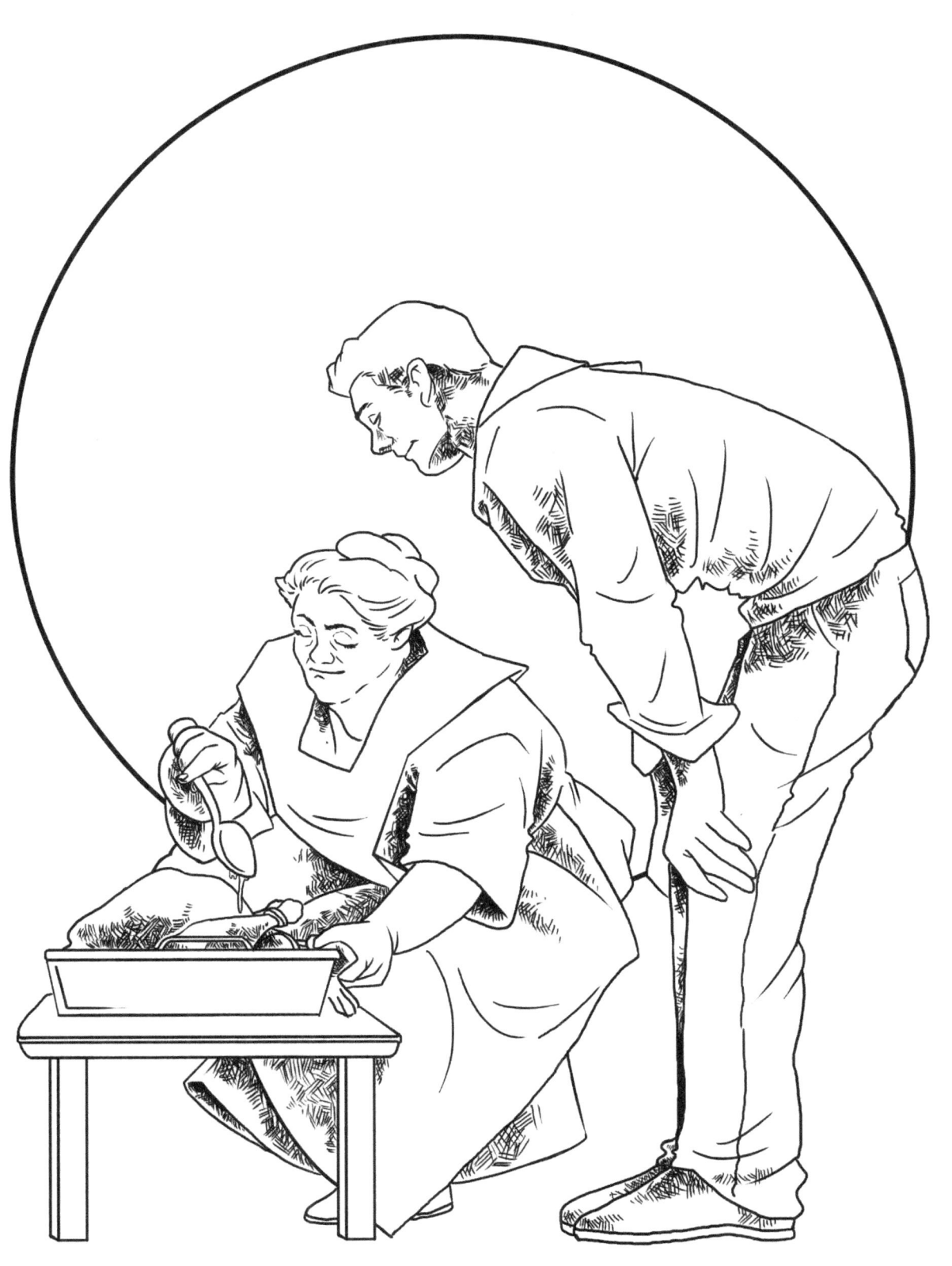

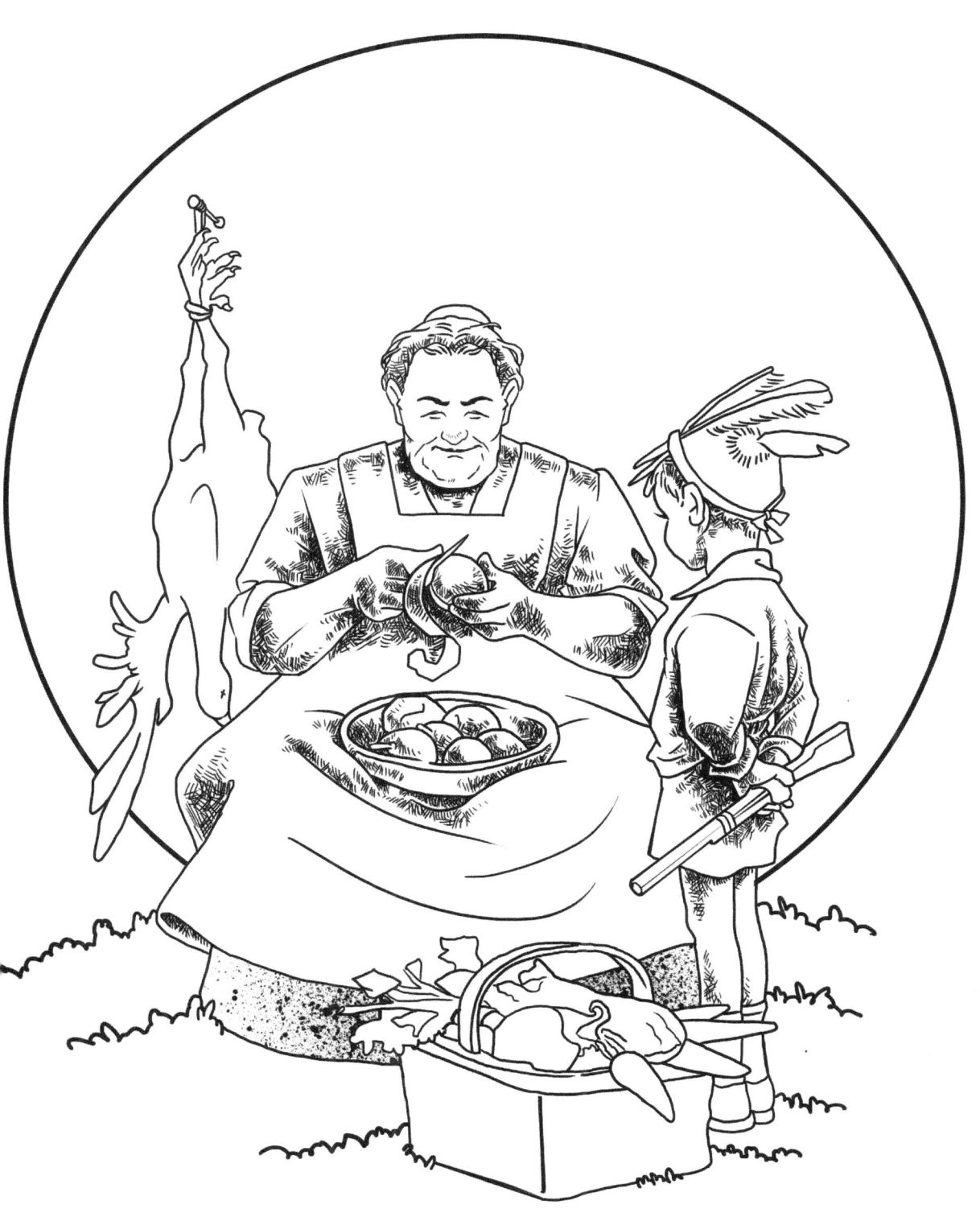

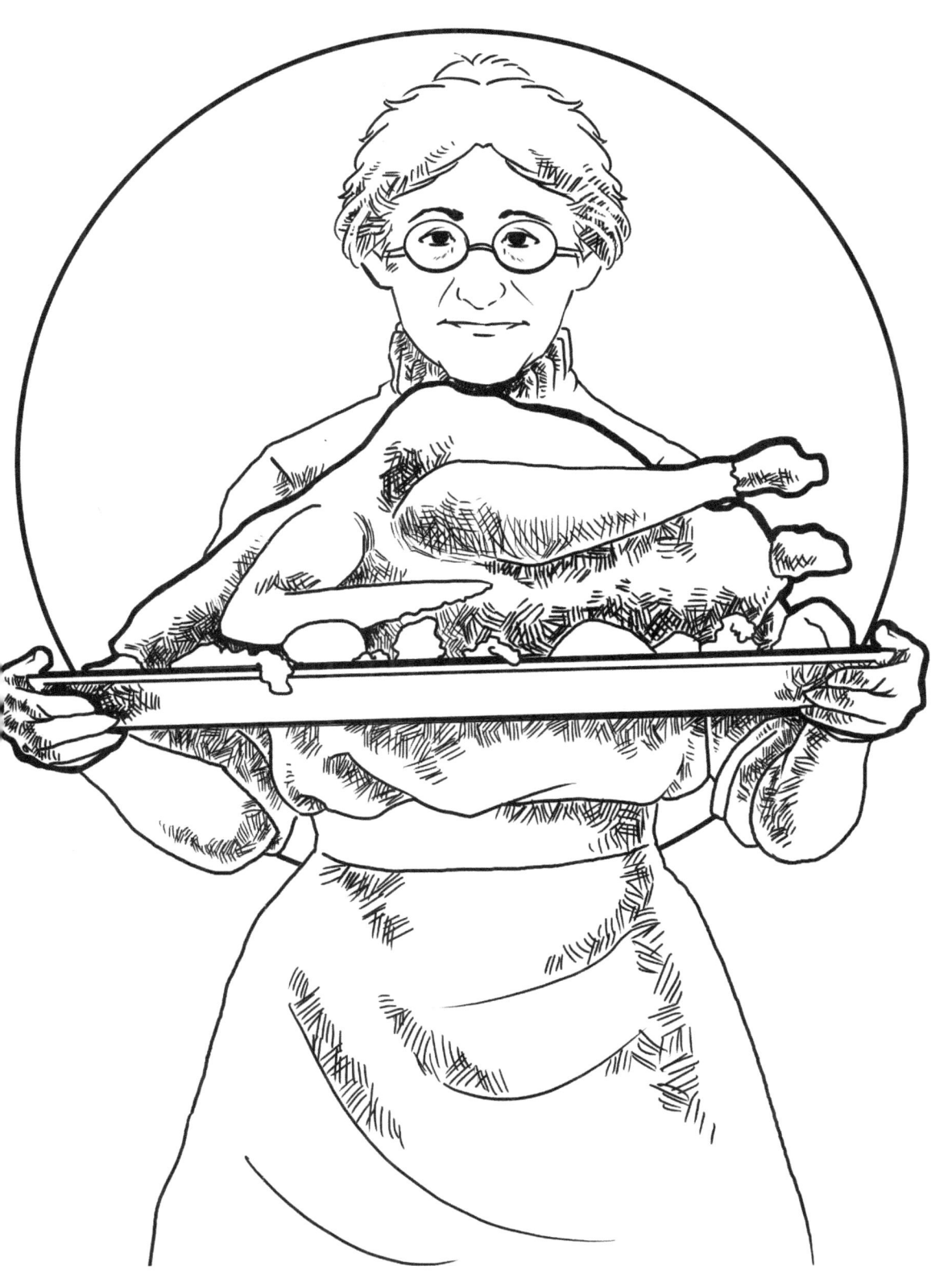

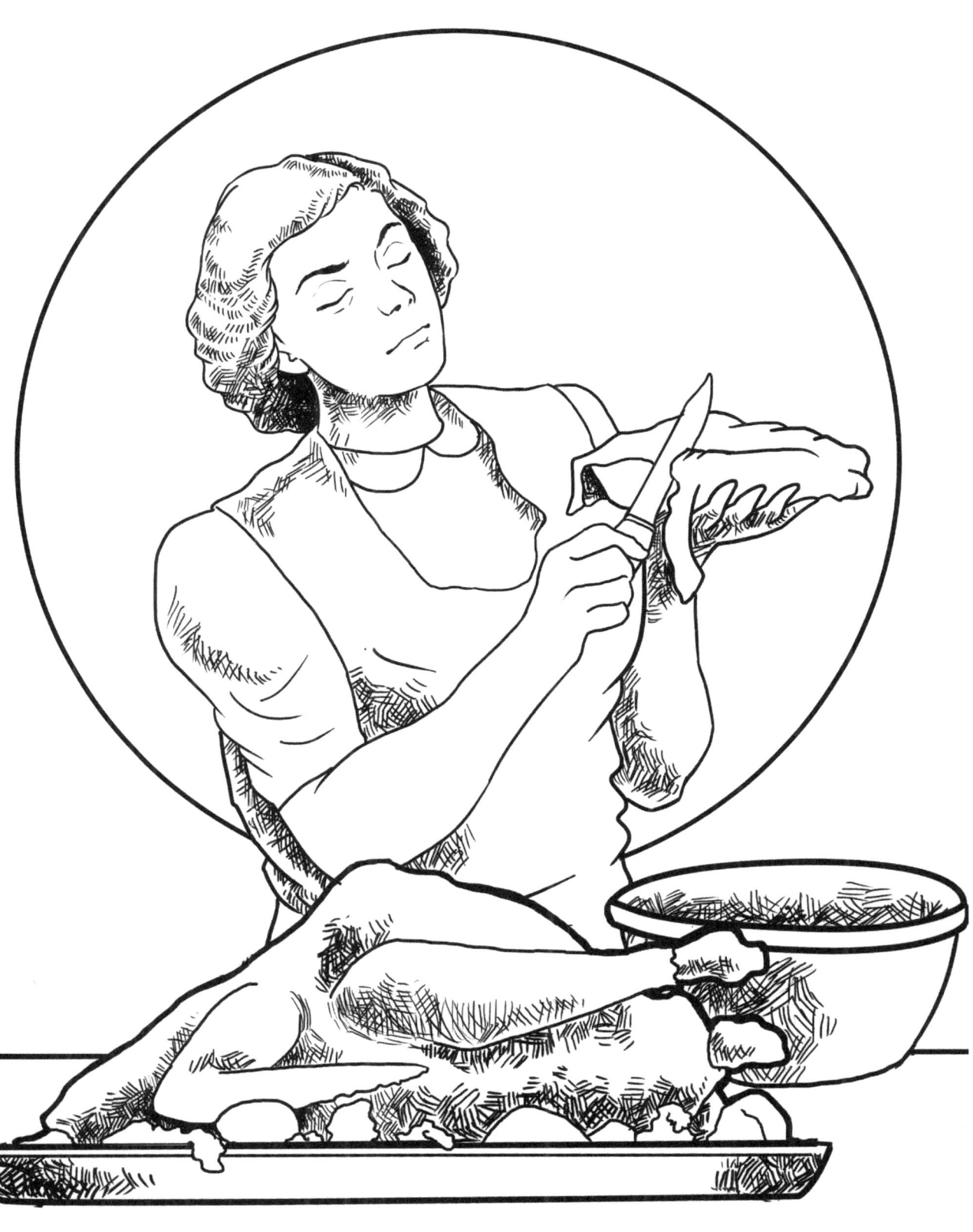

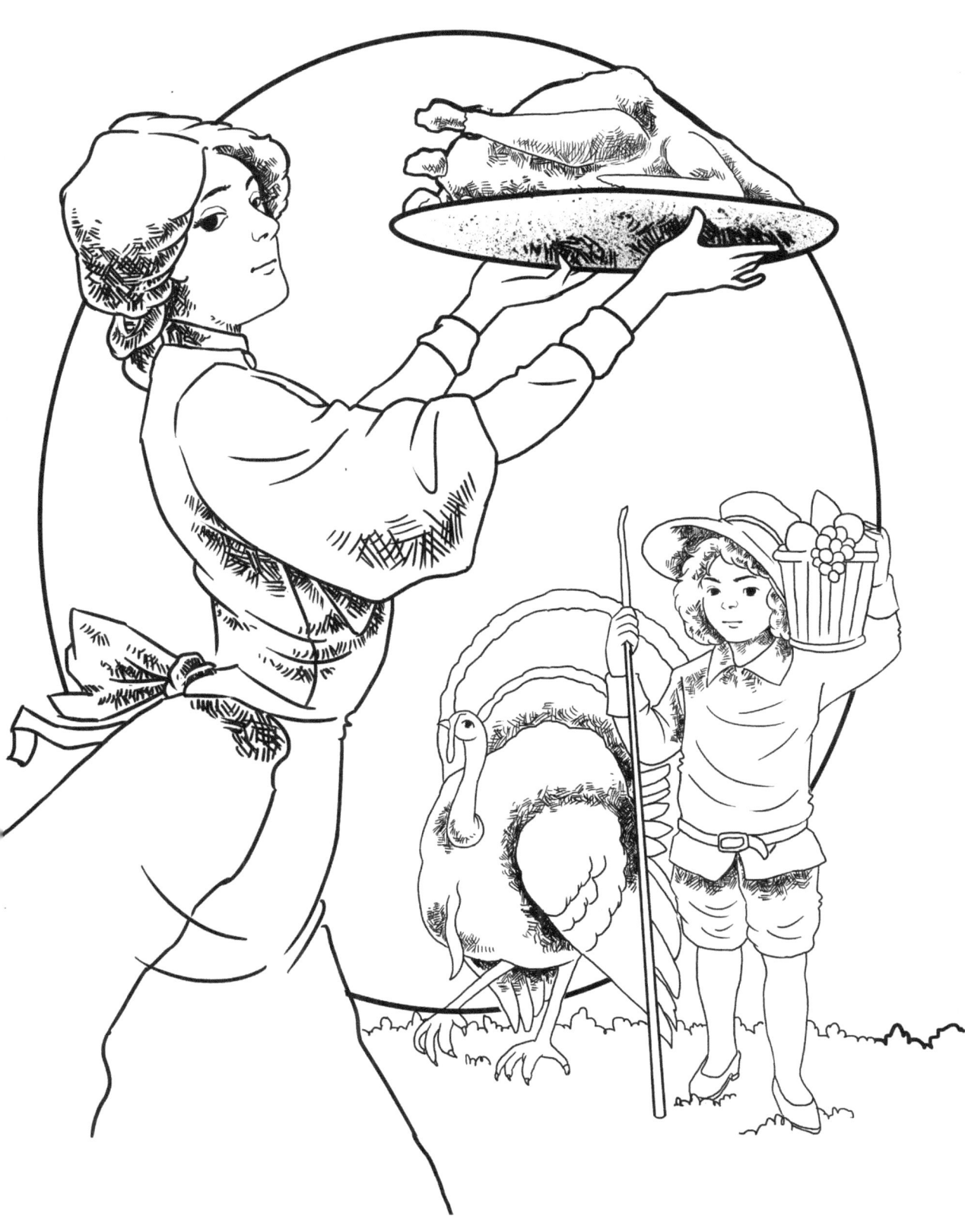

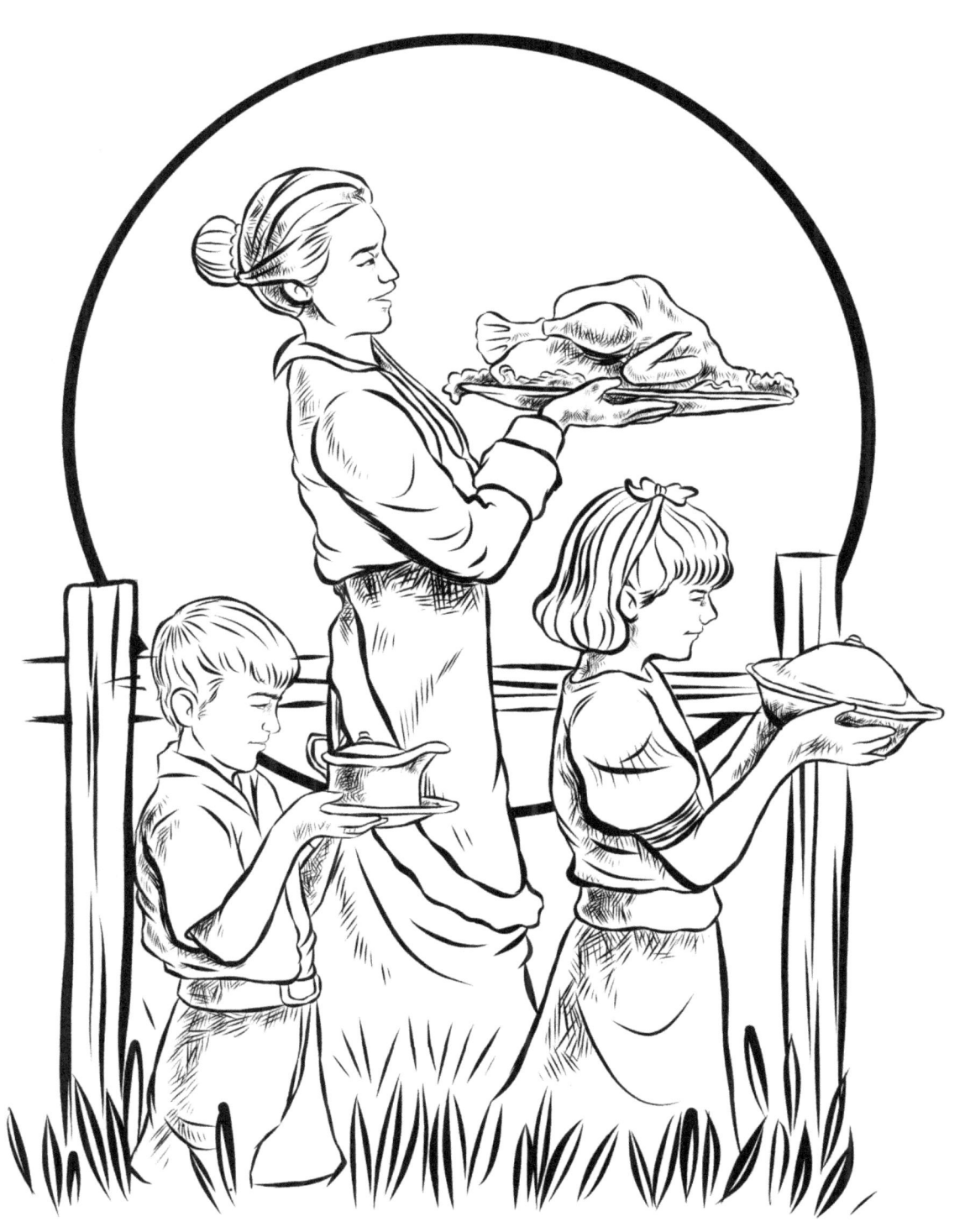

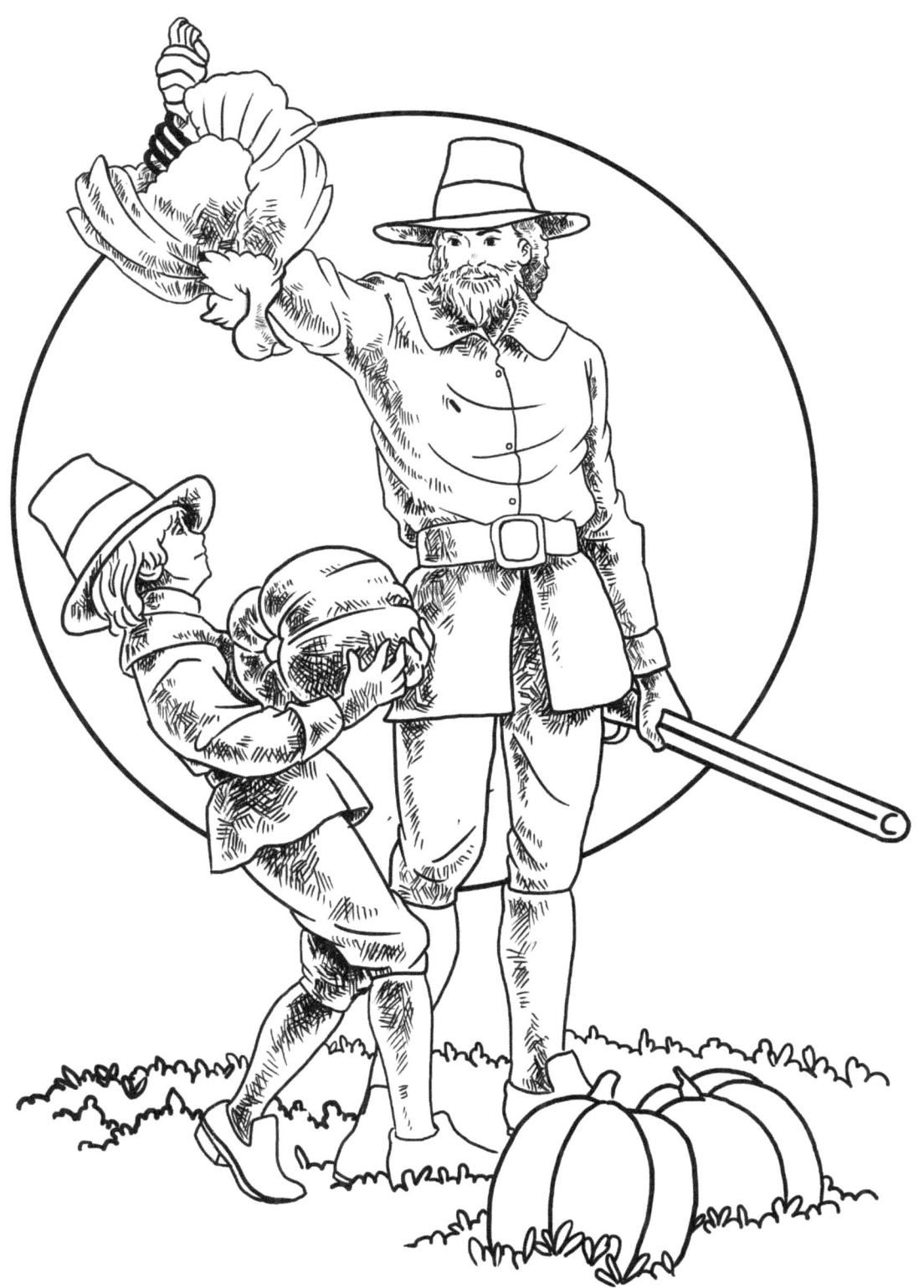

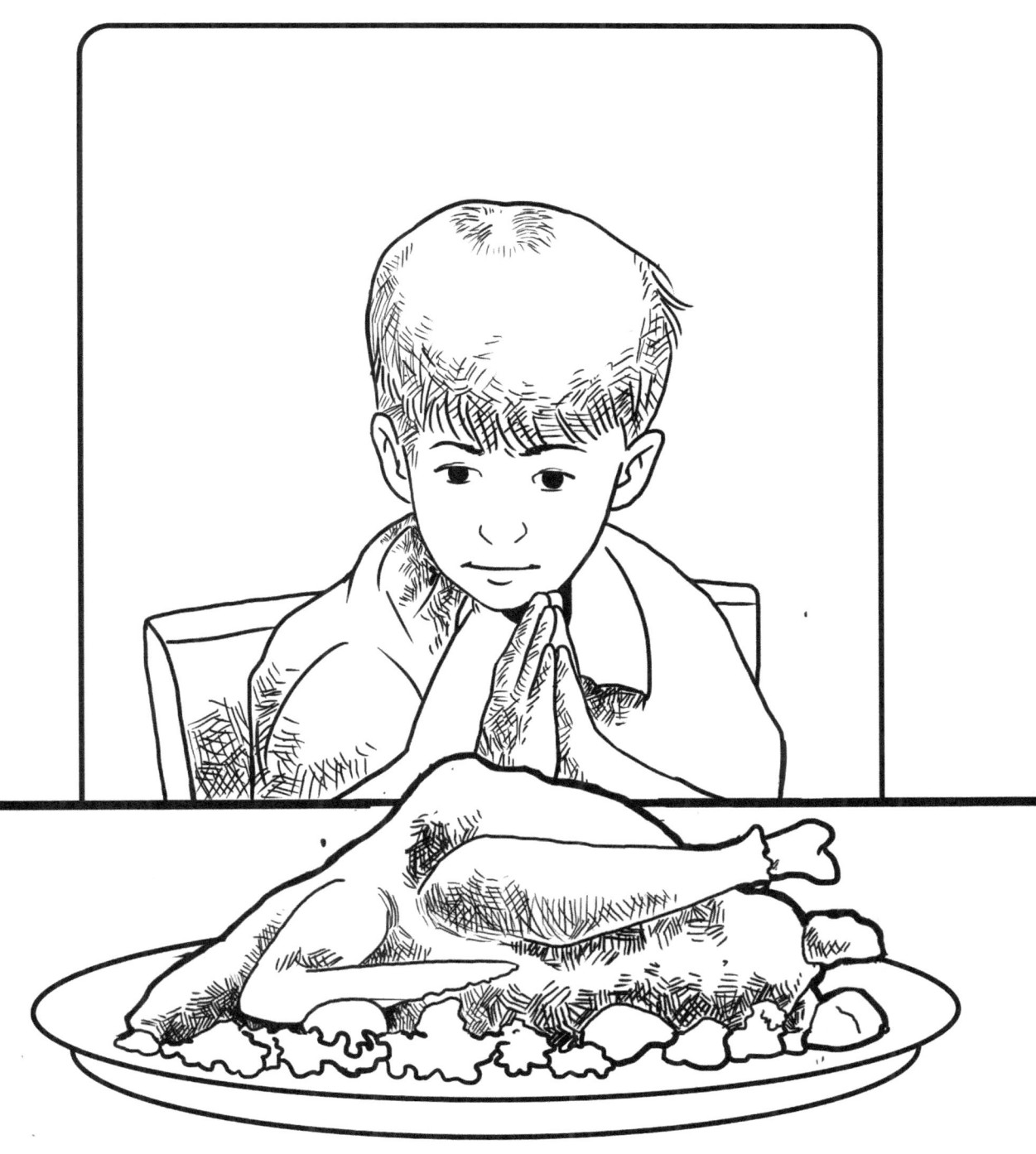

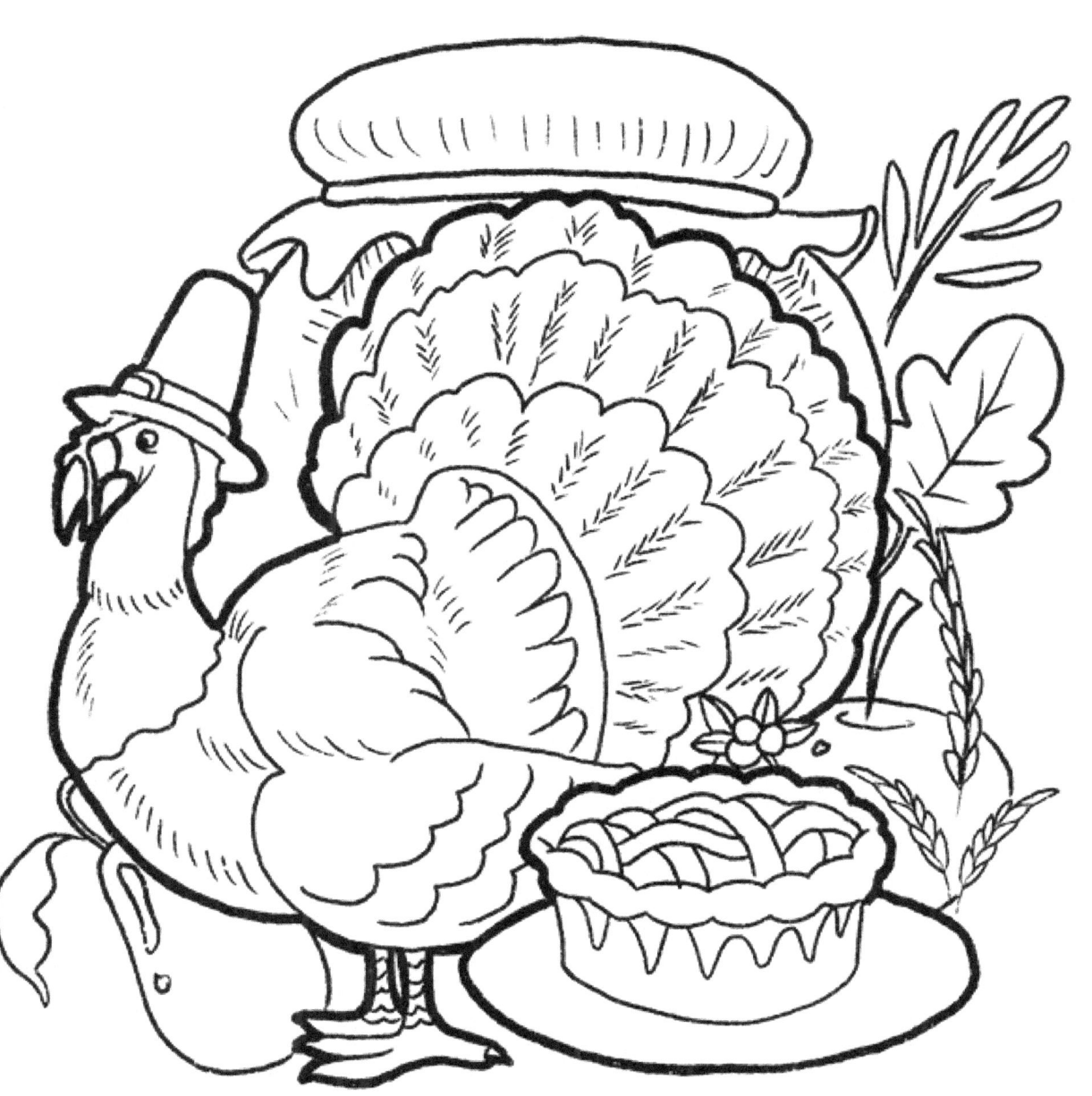

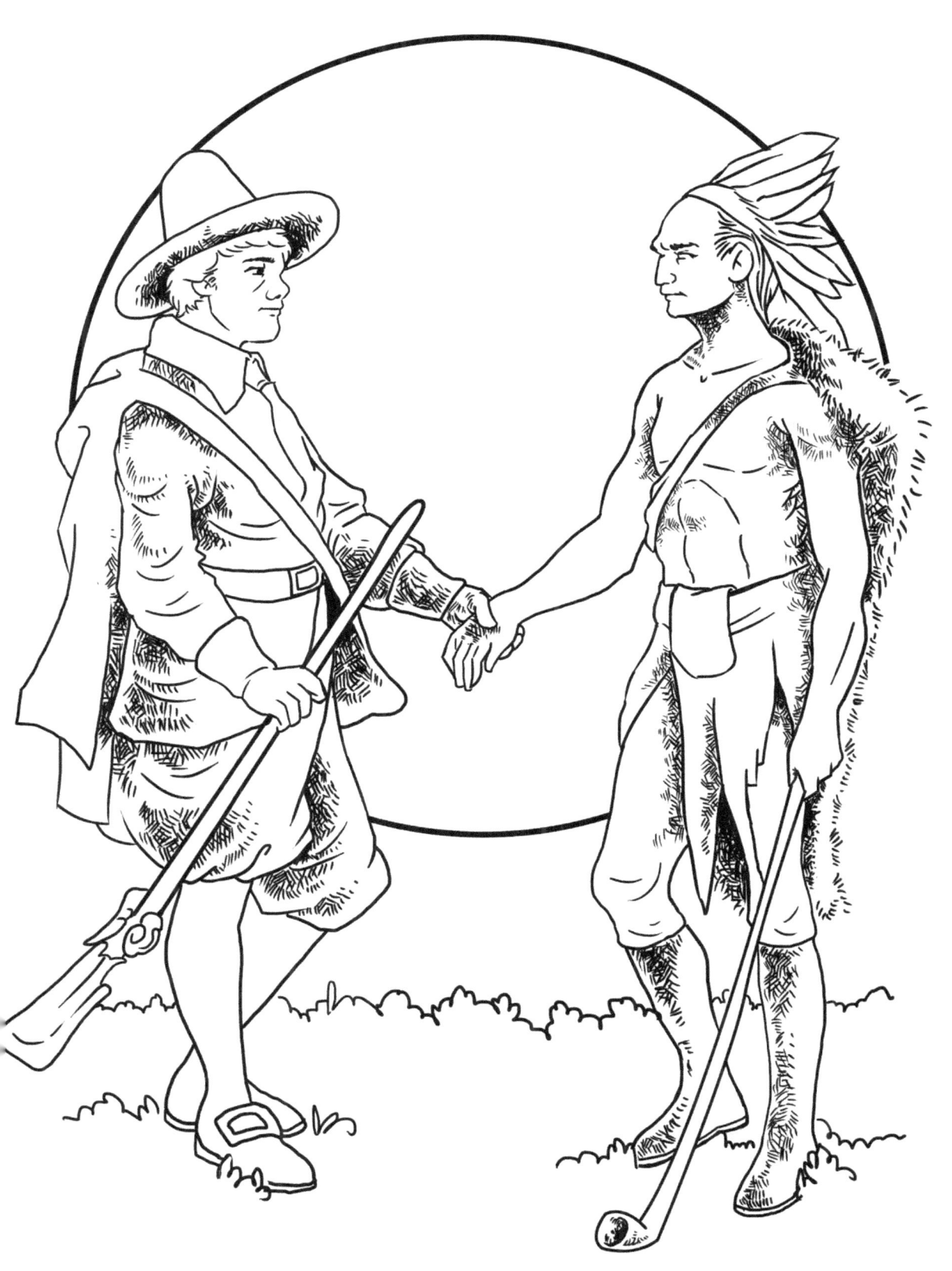

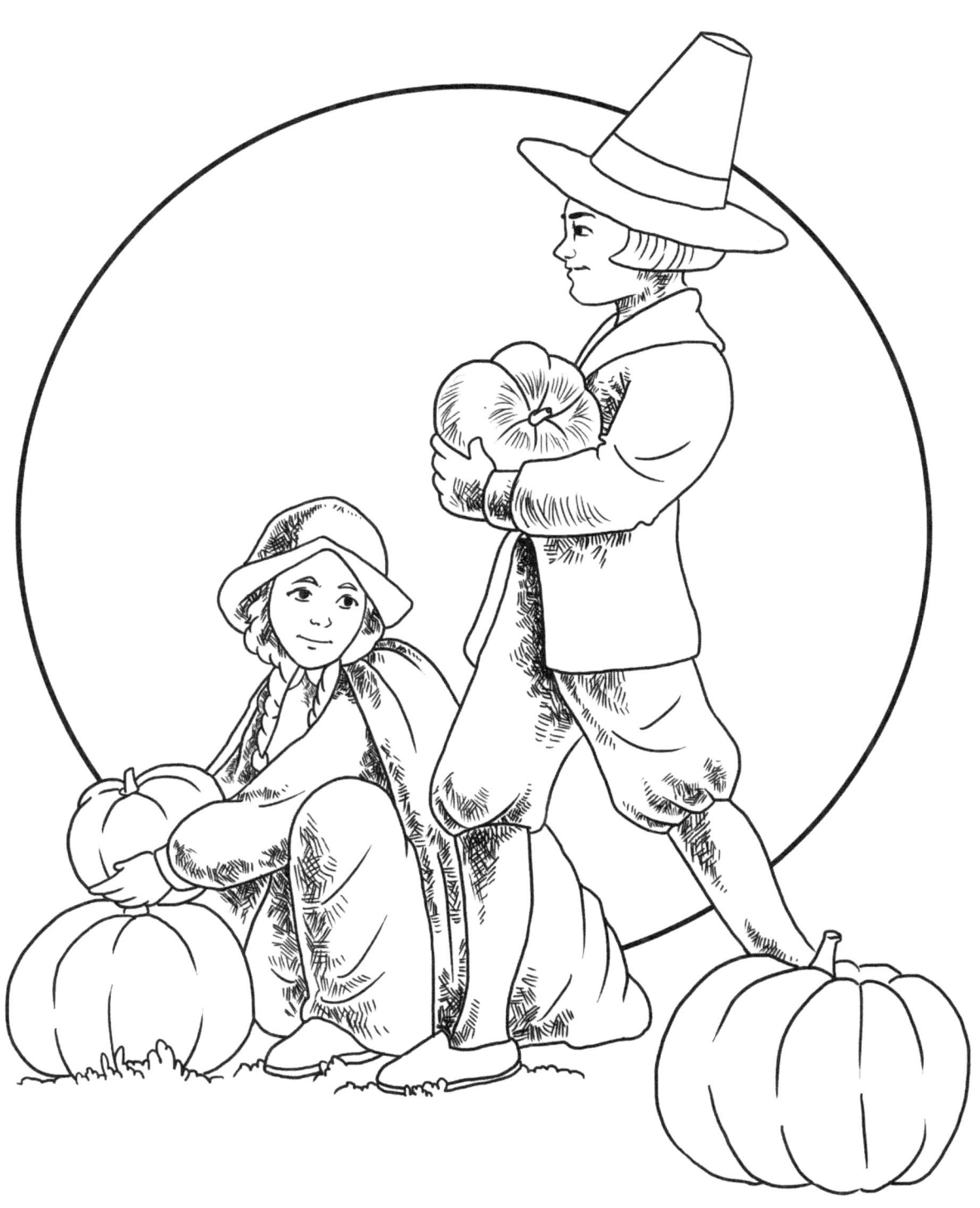

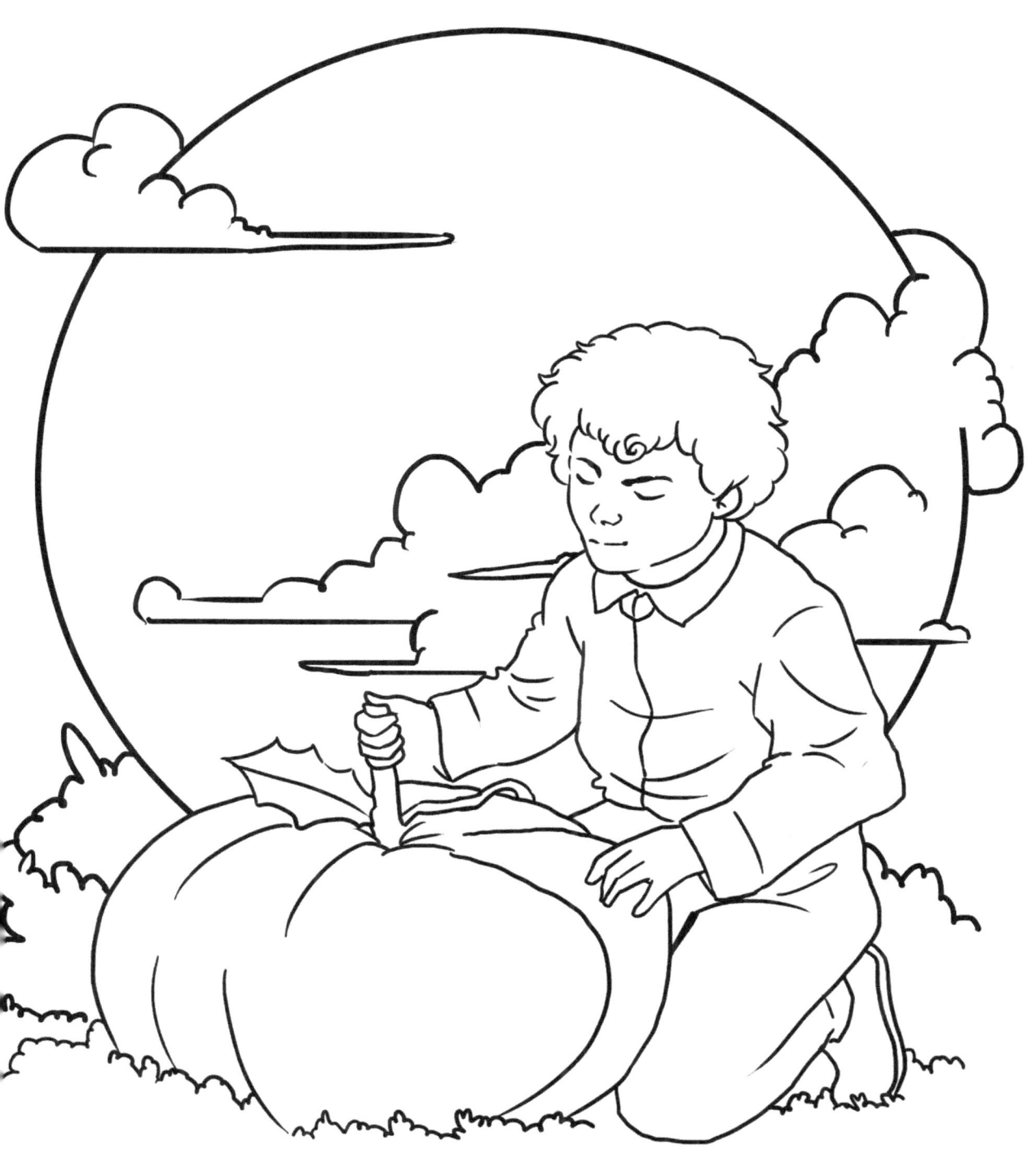

CHECK OUT OUR LATEST BOOK!

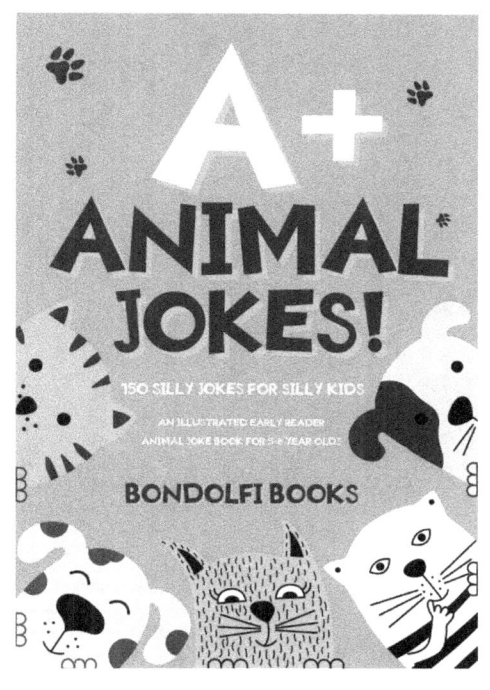

IF YOU'VE ENJOYED THE BOOK, PLEASE LEAVE A 5* REVIEW ON AMAZON - IT HELPS US MORE THAN YOU KNOW!

© BONDOLFI BOOKS

www.ingramcontent.com/pod-product-compliance
Lightning Source LLC
Chambersburg PA
CBHW080622220526
45466CB00010B/3427